*Momma said,*
## "NEVER FEEL SORRY FOR A MAN"

# *Momma said,*
# "NEVER FEEL SORRY FOR A MAN"

Feel you have been affected by your past?
Want to be set free?
Ready to give life another try?

*"Rise take up thy bed and walk"*
*John 5:8*

## RAMONA PHILLIPS

*A double minded man is unstable in all of his ways:*
*James 1:8*

authorHOUSE®

*AuthorHouse™*
*1663 Liberty Drive*
*Bloomington, IN 47403*
*www.authorhouse.com*
*Phone: 1-800-839-8640*

*First published by AuthorHouse   01/12/2012*

*ISBN: 978-1-4685-4067-3 (sc)*
*ISBN: 978-1-4685-4068-0 (hc)*
*ISBN: 978-1-4685-4066-6 (ebk)*

*Library of Congress Control Number: 2012900142*

*Printed in the United States of America*

*Any people depicted in stock imagery provided by Thinkstock are models, and such images are being used for illustrative purposes only.*
*Certain stock imagery © Thinkstock.*

*This book is printed on acid-free paper.*

*Because of the dynamic nature of the Internet, any web addresses or links contained in this book may have changed since publication and may no longer be valid. The views expressed in this work are solely those of the author and do not necessarily reflect the views of the publisher, and the publisher hereby disclaims any responsibility for them.*

# Table of Contents

# Acknowledgements

I would like to acknowledge my mother who has been in my corner although we had some tough years. She now respects me as a woman appreciates me and has stated how proud of me she is. I saw her go through hurt and disappointment yet remain tough and lean on the faith that she had. She refused to give up. I learned that strength from her. In the midst of her struggles I did not know how much she was learning. I now appreciate her words of wisdom. I hope that what I share will bless many including my own three daughters, grandchildren and son. Thanks Mom for being with me through the birth of my children and not giving up on me.

Thanks to my Pastor David Evans for all of his teachings of wisdom, knowledge and understanding and renewal of the mind. I have eaten the meat and now I am living it. Thanks also to all who have been in my corner and supported me in some way including others who I have learned from. I am still teachable. I love you all.

***Most of all I would like to say thank you to my Lord and Savior Jesus Christ who chose to give me specific gifts. I am so glad that He has kept me. I am most grateful for the opportunity to serve His Kingdom. I love you Jesus.***

Ramona

# Introduction

I felt led to write this book because of my own personal experiences in my relationships. I remember as a young girl, when my dad use to leave me in the car as he chose to go into the bar to get his drink on. I remember the fear in the darkness as I hid when men walked by the car. In the seventies I remember the disappointment when my father would say he would come to get me and never showed up. I remember yearning to be loved, I wanted to feel like daddy's girl. I remember thinking sex was love. After my first experience I did not get the message, it did not **feel** like love. What was love anyway?

My heart goes out to all the young girls and women who are still yearning for the love that they did not get from their fathers. I do understand the feelings of abandonment and anger and questioning if he really loved me. Why did drinking seem to be more important than me? I asked him not to drink many times but he would just laugh. I did not understand why he thought it was funny. I look at my own childhood and wonder why our men struggle so hard to become the men and father's that God created them to be. I see them constantly under attack but do not understand why many of them refuse to give their lives to a God who is much bigger then their pride. I don't understand why some pretend to love you just to get what they want. I don't understand why men don't see through their selfish ways into the eyes of their daughters or the woman that needs him to love her back. We keep going that extra mile for them and why? Many of them don't know what that extra mile is, giving of self unselfishly.

Why are some of us attracted to men who don't qualify to be in a relationship or who are not looking to get married? I don't understand why so many of us keep ignoring the signs. That clearly say that these men **don't know how** to love us the way we need them to. Why do we ignore the anger in them, why do we ignore the player in them? Why do we compromise our integrity and self-worth and choose not to guard our hearts? Why do we hang on until our heart can't stand the pain anymore of not letting go? Why don't we set boundaries? Why don't we set standards? I lived for many years not knowing that I needed to set standards. No one taught me. How could I make the same mistakes that my mother made after telling myself that I wouldn't?

So I came up with a plan of my own when I was about thirteen years of age. I dreamt of having a husband, I knew I needed one of those. I then would have 2 children, a girl and a boy. That sounded like the perfect family to me. My mother had had eight, that was too many for me. Besides I was helping raise them, so two sounded better. Now how was I going to make this happen? I did not know it was not my job to **Make** it happen. How many women seek the man of their dreams only ending up with the man of their nightmares? We meet men that are not healthy for us. We see that they are drinkers, druggies, liars, cheaters, abusers and many don't know how to honor a woman. Many don't know what good character and integrity mean. Many of us grew up not knowing. Let's be honest. We did learn: abuse, eating disorders, depression, confusion, rage, low self-esteem, neediness, fear, un-forgiveness and giving until it hurts and of course more trauma.

Why do we feel sorry for them? I got it. They have a sad past too. Awww. His momma or daddy was not there for him. He grew up in Foster homes, he was abused too. Why do we think we can change them? Why don't we think of the consequences if we choose to take this road? For some the consequences have even been their lives. That almost happened to me. God has been merciful to me and I am grateful.

My momma told me to never feel sorry for a man, but I chose not to listen. Maybe it was not clear to me what I was doing. Maybe I thought it was no big deal, I had things under control. Why should I listen to her, after all she chose to feel sorry for them.

I watched her as she was being abused and used, and we were in the middle of all the chaos. I watched her health seem to get worse and her blood pressure medication get increased. **Wait . . . maybe she actually learned from her pain and suffering, could this be?** I don't know, all I know is that I don't want to go on that same journey. What a childhood nightmare. Well guess what? I did not go on that journey, but I sure came close to her journey, my own nightmare.

We can learn from the pain, mistakes, bad choices, and ignorance of others. **All we need to do is ask God to remove the pride and change our hearts.** Then we can become teachable when we are willing to change. Age has nothing to do with it, many of us are little girls in the bodies of grown women. **It is time for us to realize that our perfect daddy died on the cross for us.** As far as a husband is concerned, when we are busy doing HIS work and minding our business and not looking for a man. Our perfect Father will surprise us with a man that not only loves us but loves Him as well. No peeking. Well you can turn the pages of this book to take a look at my story.

# Chapter 1

## In the Beginning was the *TEEN YEARS*

I was seventeen years old living in North Philadelphia in an abandoned house; well actually, it was a condemned house. We were heart broken when my mother said we had to move from our home near 38th and Girard. She tried to cover it up by telling us she had a disagreement with the landlord Ms. Chase. The house did need some ceiling work, but in reality it was because she could not pay the rent. I was taking classes at the time, and working at Gino's. (a.k.a. now KFC).

Myself, my mother three brothers and three sisters had no place else to go except this condemned house. Well that is what my mother thought. A relative whom we had never met owned the house as we were told. I remember when we got there, a so called boyfriend of mine who had introduced me to my first taste of monster(speed)had helped us move. I never put it in my nose, only my tongue. That experience only lasted a few weeks. I got tired of it challenging me when I wanted to get some sleep. God's grace would not allow me to be a drug addict.

I still remember the the hurt on my little brother's face, as he was told to help pull off the aluminum siding from the windows. I noticed the orange sticker from the city that was proof the house was not livable. You are probably wondering why were we living in a house not fit for anyone to live in? We were forced to move out of our home after my mother's gambling debts had to take priority over the bookies who had threaten to break her legs. My mother had been gambling since we were little children, not every day. It was her plan to get extra money when the money was running out.

She managed to keep food on the table and was a good cook. We hated the gambling habit. She worked sometimes as a nurse's aide or at the candle factory. But raising 7 children alone was difficult. I guess she felt that hitting the number would help, and strangely at times she would hit and it did bring in some extra money. But most times she didn't.

Some time later, I had a minimum wage job at an insurance company in Center City Philadelphia after taking some keypunch classes. I called it my first real job after working in fast food restaurants during my early teen years and cleaning the meat man's home for Trans Pass money to go to school.

I had no belief at the time that I could go to college. Dreams and goals were never discussed in our home. Nor was I affirmed as to how special I was. I was self motivated by what I already knew or hoped for. I thought middle-class or rich people could only go to college. I wanted to be a nurse but felt my family did not have the money so those dreams went out of the window.

I got paid bi-weekly and hated the fact that my mother would make me feel guilty until she got at least half my paycheck. We had agreed on a specific amount and I honored that. I loved my mother a lot, but I just wanted to see her make better choices. I wanted her to show me appreciation.

I wanted a better life. I was tired of the insanity in our home. Later after the water was shut off we had to borrow water from the neighbor and the kitchen was shut off with a board in the doorway, because of the rats. My mother cooked on a hot plate in the dining room, she sank into depression. The rooms were always dark except for a little light coming in from a open curtain.

I would come home from work everyday and play one of my albums and just dance myself tired until I was ready to go to sleep. That was something I was good at, even dancing in school. But when I got to high school I did not have the confidence to resume a career in the Arts. Nor did I know anything about Performing Arts School. I loved drama, dance, singing and playing the violin.

My sister and I use to perform in middle school. We both played the violin, danced and sang in our younger years. It was a few good memories I have from my childhood. Dancing was also a way to keep warm in that cold little house. Remember The Jackson Five, Earth Wind and Fire, Teddy Pendergrass, the Ohio Players, Heatwave? Now that was music.

After dancing, and bathing in cold water, well sometimes if I wanted to wait I would heat the water on the hotplate. I would then put on my mohair nightgown that I got from the thrift store to keep me warm and get on the sofa bed in the living room. We had electric but no heat. We had to bathe upstairs in a cold room after the bathroom sink and tub stopped working. We would never allow any friends to come in to use our toilet.

We all had our way of coping. Some did drugs, some drank, some looked for others in relationships to rescue them. I had done enough drugs and alcohol by the age of nineteen to last me a while including selling speed(yellow jacks, christmas trees)in capsules on the street to friends, just for $2 a piece for lunch money.

Strangely, I loved angle dust; it smelt like peppermint. A so called boyfriend introduced this green stuff to me. When smoking it, I felt I was standing high off the ground as if wearing elevator shoes. During those Summer nights, I would look up at the sky at the stars and just wish I could reach up and touch it. I was too ignorant and immature at the time to know that I was doing a drug that was very dangerous.

I still can't believe I was doing these things at such a young age, it was my way of escape.

I watched my mother in and out of abusive relationships every since I was a little girl in elementary school. I watched my mother feel sorry for each of these sick men. **In my earlier teen years, there were three that were the most insane.**

The first one was Mr. Walt short, stocky built and probably never stepped foot in a gym. He had a cool walk and a swag that got most people's attention. And Mr. Kenny, red bone skin tone with a dual personality. He would change from a perm to an afro so quick you would wonder if his real name was Clark Kent. He would look in the mirror after changing his hair and admire himself.

My sister and I would peek at him when the bathroom door was open and watch him talking to himself as if in love with himself. At the time I did not understand what vanity meant. He would say to himself "I am a pretty motherf____. You know the word. My sister, and I were fifteen months apart and close. We were the two oldest girls, I was the oldest. We did a lot of praying together in those days. We learned how to pray until we got a answer. We prayed a lot out of fear.

When my mother tried to break up with Mr. Walt, he threatened to kill her. He told her if he couldn't have her nobody else would have her. One night when we were in our beds on the third floor(another home of course) I heard my mother screaming, my name I believe. Her room was at the bottom of the stairs, I woke up and went to her room. She was lying on the bed bleeding and screaming in pain and fear. Mr. Walt had followed her home and stabbed her three times.

I called the police and she was taken to the hospital, he had missed her heart by inches. She survived. All was well for a short period of time, maybe a few weeks, until one night, we were sleep in our rooms. We were awaken by loud glass breaking downstairs. We ran upstairs to the third floor where my aunt and her children slept.

We were afraid to go downstairs. There was an evil presence in the house. We began to smell smoke coming up the stairs, we ran down the stairs. We were trapped on the second floor. Mr. Walt had broken in the house placed the trash bags of trash on the steps and set them on fire and ran out.

At the time my cousin was living with us. He leaped over the banister, and ran out of the house, the fire department was arriving around the same time. Fortunately we lived near the fire station. Seven children my mother my aunt and her two children, trapped in a three story house saved just in time. Thank God. Someone must have been praying for us. I believe it was my mother's oldest sister, some great aunts and my grandmother and relatives on my father's side.

You would think that experience would have been enough, of course not. I mentioned Mr. Kenny remember? My mother met him some time after Mr. Walt. One day while we were in the bedroom watching Soul Train, my mother and Mr. Kenny was arguing on the stairs. I peeked out the room, and he had a large butcher knife in his hand. He was threatening my mother with it and hitting the wall. Being the oldest, I felt a strange sense of responsibility for my family.

5

I felt I had to do something. When I got the chance and saw an opening between the two, I ran down the stairs and just as I hit the front door, he said "get back up here before I kill your mother"! His voice was very threatening. At first I looked at the door wondering if I should take a chance and run and get help. But I was afraid that I would come back and everyone would be dead.

I would have felt it was my fault. Going back could not have been the best choice, but I took the chance. Slowly I came back up the stairs keeping my eyes on him and my mother, hoping he would not plunged the knife in my back. I was maybe 11 years old at the time.

My mother was able to calm him down. We were able to relax a little as they went in the other room. Some days later, I do remember he turned into a copy cat psycho. One night while we were sleeping, once again we heard a loud noise downstairs. We smelt smoke and ran down the stairs. Mr. Kenny had set the trash on fire in the kitchen. Once again saved by divine intervention.

It looked as if Mr. Kenny and my mother had split up for good. I thought she had pressed charges on him. We moved a short time after to a house in West Philadelphia, things were looking up. It was like the Jefferson's. I felt we were moving on up. We had a better house with seven bedrooms 2 bathrooms, shed kitchen, three floors and new friends. Uncle Jim, my mother's uncle came to live with us some time later.

My mother started seeing Mr. Kenny again briefly. I don't know how he found us and why she started seeing him again. It was not before long when his old ways began to show up again. He and my mother got into another argument. He had her trapped in the stairway with a knife. I know, again.

One time, I remember my sister and I were in the trash house out in the back yard, it use to be an outhouse I guess, but we used it for trash bags. I remember standing on top of these trash bags hoping we had enough space to not be found. We would go some place to hide and pray whenever things got too crazy.

One time, Uncle Jim was in his room but we thought he was out. We were praying continuously that Uncle Jim would show up and help us. We heard a noise in the kitchen, somebody went in the kitchen. I felt like I was in a "Lifetime" movie. We did not want to leave that trash house but was not sure if the person who had took something out of the kitchen was coming after us. Of course we were suffering from traumatic stress disorder but did not know it. I think my little brothers and sisters were all outside at the time afraid to come in the house.

Then we decided to go inside to see what was going on. My uncle Jim had heard my mother screaming, he was a big man over six feet tall husky. He came downstairs with a hammer and was hitting Mr. Kenny over and over again in his head. OMG! We were relieved and terrified at the same time! He ran out the door and I believe my mother felt sorry for him and got him some help. I am not sure if she went to the hospital with him. Of course, he had the nerve to come back.

Later that night, my mother had gone a few houses down at Pop and Sis's house.a The neighbors would go to their home to hang out and have a few drinks. My sister and I were in our room on the second floor trying to get to sleep after such a traumatic day. Then suddenly we heard Mr. Kenny calling my mother. The door must have been unlocked. He was coming up the stairs. He walked through the door of our room with a big bandage on his head asking where was my mother. OMG! Where was my mother?

My sister and I leaped on one side of the bed near the door, as he walked around the other side of our bed. We ran out of the room upstairs to tell Uncle Jim. Mr. Kenny went looking for her. I believe he found her. Uncle Jim did not seem to care when we asked for his help. He stayed in his room. At the time I did not understand why he did not come to rescue us this time. He was probably disappointed that my mother had felt sorry for him and helped him. Or at least that's what it looked like. We were getting mixed messages.

We were very disappointed, what next? The fear was so overwhelming for me that I grew numb. I don't remember what happened next. I know that they finally broke up for good. I believe she finally sent him away for good.

But then a few weeks later, my mother got a visit from some detectives while we were in school. When we got home she told us that she heard that Mr. Kenny had stabbed some women with 8 kids 30 something times. Her oldest son discovered her body. OMG! He had murdered someone's mother! We did not need to hear that. So fear and trauma was back. Is he coming to get us too? Can we move? What should we do? We had better watch our backs.

We were glad that he was no where in sight. But It was hard sleeping and finding peace most days. It was hard playing outside not knowing if he was going to turn the corner. Did black people get therapy during those days? Only crazy ones ... right? Ignorance. At least that is how we thought back then when we would see the white woman on TV running off to see her therapist. Like I said, Ignorance.

A few weeks later, after he had killed that poor woman and her son had found her, my sister and I were on 52nd and Girard and there he was. OMG! Mr. Kenny was walking down 52nd street, thank God, he did not see us. He had on those same clothes from weeks ago. He was walking like a zombie.

We ran to the pay phone and called to warn my mother, cause he was walking in the same direction as our home. She answered the phone and said that he was at the door. He was pushing the door to get in.

She climbed on the roof, we entered, our block from another direction. We saw the police patty wagon pull up in front of our house. We ran down and stopped them, and told them what we knew. They said that they had him in the wagon. What a relief, maybe this nightmare was finally over. My mother said he looked up at her when the police arrived and said thank you. Wow. We never saw him again, this was in 1975 I believe. I felt so sorry for the woman that was killed and her grieving children. I also felt grateful that she was not my mother and I had not been the one that found her.

Unfortunately, there is one more. We called him "Fonz" because he wore a short leather jacket and had a goofie swag. Maybe he was a fan of "The Fonz" on Happy Days. He was younger than my mother. He was my friend's big brother who had just come home from the Military. They dated for some months, then he wanted to move in with us.

My mother said no, although she did not tell us everything that was going on. We later found out how unstable he was. Actually, he use to come around when we were hanging out with our friends on the steps or something. He always looked so strange, and very quiet and seem to be watching everyone. I still don't trust people who are known to be very quiet.

Uncle Jim was no longer living with us, now uncle Cornelius was. He was not like Uncle Jim. He later disappeared and they found him on the bus, he had had a heart attack. We never saw him again. I believe his body was sent back down south and we could not attend the funeral.

My mother realized something was not stable about Fonz and tried to break up with him. Strange things began to happen in the house. Actually, that feeling of not feeling safe in our own home, came back. At least that was my perception.

One night, there were some wires hanging from the basement ceiling. My mother told us and I felt something was not right. We were running in and out of the house at the time, my brothers and sisters were much younger. I was fifteen years old now. Most times the door was unlocked.

Then on October 13th 1976, I came in the house, I heard a noise at the top of the stairs where our room was. It sounded like someone was doing something they should not be doing and heard me come in. I went up the stairs, Fonz was in our room. I asked him why was he snooping around in my room. I was a direct girl and still the same today. He gave me a strange look and did not answer my question.

He actually, changed the subject. He asked me a question about a picture or something on the wall. I continued to ask him why was he snooping around in my room. He walked out and went down the stairs and left. I looked around in the room to see if anything was missing. I felt he had been in the area where the window was but could not make any sense out of it at the time.

The next night, October 14th, I came home early that evening to dye my trench coat baby blue and get some rest for school. I had been messing up and needed to regroup. I went to sleep not even hearing when my sister came in and got in the bed with me. While I was sleeping on my stomach my body almost jumped off of the bed. I awoke instantly and heard a noise coming from my neck. It was a spitting sound. I took my right hand and felt my neck, I was bleeding. I sat on the edge of the bed and put on my slippers and shook my sister. She always slept hard, she did not awake.

I looked over at the window and it was open. I knew we never left the window open. I heard **something** inside of me say "go wake up your mother". I walked toward the door, unlocked it and walked down the hall to knock on my mother's door. I began to knock hard. She opened it and asked what happened to me.

I could not speak because of the bleeding. She grabbed me and we ran across the street to the night club called "1990". A few people were coming out. My mother was screaming, "somebody did something to my daughter"! Please help us! A light skinned man and a woman put me in a small car and started driving very fast. By this time I was vomiting blood, my clothes were drenched with blood down to my panties.

My mother ran home to take the children to the neighbors while this man was trying to save my life. Meanwhile, I later heard that she ran into Fonz. He was never up after 11 p.m. because he worked on the ship and had to get up early. She felt something was not right but could not put her hands on it at the time. She told him what happened and he helped her get the kids to his apartment, which was a few doors down. My brother said that he noticed that he was changing his boots quickly.

When I got there the hospital staff was waiting and got me to the ER and I heard them say we have to get her into surgery. They were rushing me down the hall, and I saw my mother, they stopped briefly. She said, "are you alright"? I signaled "are you alright"? Amazing, I should have been praying silently or thinking of myself.

Eight hours of surgery, and waking up slowly with my hands tied to the bed and my neck bandaged up and two detectives waiting for me to awake. I regained consciousness; tears streamed down my face as I wondered what had happened to me. The detectives started questioning me. I did not know nor did I understand who would do such a terrible thing to me.

I was glad to be alive although I could not speak and had a tube in my throat for three weeks. The Dr's said that I may have to go home with the tube in my windpipe and I may not be able to speak again because of a fractured vocal cord. Well today, I am speaking and I did not have to go home with that tube in my windpipe although my vocal cord is still slightly fractured. I still love to sing and whistle. Yes, whistle. It helps keep the mind in a positive place. Try it.

While I was in the hospital my mother received sympathy cards in the mail expressing sorrow for my death. Mother realized that Fonz was involved and there was some confrontation, but it needed to be settled in court. She decided to move to another house so I would not have to go back to the same house. My mother and I went back and forth to court. We would some times run into him in the hall and he would say nothing to us. Nothing . . .

I sometimes wondered why he did not come to me and plead his innocence. My wishful thinking I guess. His brother and I were friends, and he decided to take his brother's side so we stopped speaking. I figured he had to know that his brother was sick, but he did not see it that way. I know blood is thicker than water, but truth is more important to me, I don't care who it is.

One night, my brother's girlfriend and I were going to the store, we were living on a little block called Cambridge Street just a few blocks from the Philadelphia Zoo. We were walking and talking, then we saw a car that looked like Fonz's car creeping up on us really slow. We ran and hid, it was him. He had followed my little brother home from school and found out where we lived. We ran home and told my mother, she called the police and then she got a restraining order. This seemed to help keep him away.

I wondered what his plans was, I shutter to think that he was coming to finish me off. OMG! It was difficult and hard getting on that witness stand and being treated as if I was the criminal instead of the victim. Long story short, I felt as if the law was telling me that I had no value or rights because I was no longer a virgin. I was once involved with Fonz's brother, you know the friend I mentioned?

What does one thing have to do with the other? Didn't I deserve justice? Fonz did not do a day in jail. I guess him being in the Military gave him more favor in the eyes of the law or Government, than I had. My so called country had let me down.

It was said that all the evidence was substantial that also included: the foot prints that were found in the back yard and ship nail with blood on it (which could have been used to puncture the 3 wholes that were in my neck and shoulder)that was found in the trunk of his car. And his paranoia in the hospital waiting room and him being up late that night. Well, where was Perry Mason, Kojak, Madlock now? Supreme Court? Yea right!

Wow, on TV he would have been sent to jail for a long time. Where was the justice for this fifteen year old girl who had been through so much already? All of this had added to the trauma and pain that I had already gone through. I grew up with some anger towards my mother and with men as a young girl. I did not trust them although I still managed to have relationships with them. Then of course the cycle continued with me, well sort of.

By age 18 when my mother tried to give me advice about a man of course I would never listen. She would later say "never feel sorry for a man." It never occurred to me that she was actually learning from her experiences. I was arrogant, rebellious, stubborn, and resentful to name a few. I was also sad and afraid, lonely and lost. Usually feeling hopeless about life, and feeling stuck.

I had self—esteem issues and use to compare myself to others, although never jealous of them. At some point I believed that God would do for me what He did for people who had more than I had, I only wanted to know when. I had received Christ as Lord and Savior before I was 12.

But I was still lost. I did not know how to change my circumstances. I did not know how to change my life or myself. I never wanted to make the same choices my mother made especially when I had children. I felt abandoned by my father who was an alcoholic, I always felt sorry for him, he looked lost, and sad most of the time. He never abused my mother as she said. She said, he was afraid of her.

I was grateful to hear that, considering she had had her share of abusive men. I went to church sometimes but I was very religious. I did not know that God loved me and wanted a personal relationship with me. I was hoping to stay out of Hell. I thought God was mad at me cause I just could not seem to stop doing wrong things. I decided to get baptised around age nineteen but after leaving the church, I smoked a joint and spent a lot of time feeling guilty and condemned after that.

# Chapter 2

## Seven Years and Not married!!

***I thought an older man would treat me better.***

At age nineteen we were living in that condemned house I told you about earlier in my story, back in 1980. My father was in the hospital with mouth cancer. I decided to go visit him after leaving the gym. I actually, thought I was overweight then. I was looking good at a size 7 from a size 10. I had on royal blue carpenter jeans with my candies with low heels and a blue and yellow top. When I got to the hospital I took the elevator to his room.

There was a man in the elevator with a beautiful smile and chip tooth. He was older than me but short and taller than I was. He had on a hospital uniform. He introduced himself and you know he gave me his little rap like men do. I had no phone at home, so he gave me his home number. Eventually, we started going on dates just hanging out, and every time he tried to come in my house I would make up an excuse. He lived with his mother, he had just split up with another woman who was older than I was. He was the oldest of six brothers and sisters. He was a ex marine and twenty six years old.

One time I finally let him in the living room and put on some music, then he had to go to the bathroom and I lied and said someone was in there. We hung out most of the time or stayed in a cheap hotel. Then we decided to move in together. We started looking for a place. We found out one of his mother's relatives had a house that was not being used. We decided to ask his mother about the house. It was a three story house, and vacant. We asked if we could stay on the 2nd floor. She said yes, I went home, got some trash bags and told my mother I was moving out. Just like that. I knew at age nineteen she could not stop me.

She later wrote a letter to him accusing him of stealing her daughter away from her. I am sure she said more things he was not pleased about, I was embarrassed. I refuse to allow her to control me anymore. He saved the letter for a rainy day. Whenever he wanted to pick an argument with me he would pull out the letter and question me about what she had said. We would argue and I would tell him to ask her. I thought older guys were more mature. But then again, twenty six is still young and as I said I was nineteen.

I knew before we got together he had two ex-girlfriends that he seemed to care deeply for. He still had some past grief about Kathy. I believe he told me that she had overdosed on purpose. I am not sure if that was true or just his perception. He seemed to carry confusion and guilt from that relationship.

He use to talk about Tammy Terrell as if he knew her. So I kinda pictured Kathy that way. Then there was Pat the older one, she broke up with him for whatever reasons. He seemed to still have some unfinished business emotionally with both of them. From time to time he would compare me to them, if I did not behave the way he thought I should act in certain situations. He blamed me for everything. He was emotionally abusive and sometimes would choke me even when I was pregnant. So is this love? **Momma**

**said, "Never feel sorry for a man who has unfinished business with his ex". He may abuse you too."**

A few years later I was already beginning to regret being in the relationship. After two miscarriages and finally have given birth to a beautiful little girl I thought I was happy. I still had to accept the fact that I was with a man that drank too much. My little brother needed a place to stay, he was trying to finish school without losing his mind in that condemned house. He said, my mother did not have the money to keep him in school so he could graduate.

We decided to allow him to stay with us and we helped him finish high school. We had to put him out after he left the door open and our 6 mos. old daughter fell down the stairs in her walker. She had a dent in her forehead, but no concussion. But my boyfriend was angry with me and my brother for a long time. Funny, I guess he forgot she was my daughter my and brother's niece. We all loved her. **Momma said, "never feel sorry for a man he may be irrational".**

She seemed to develop asthma by age 2 and I spent some years running back and forth to the ER with her. This went on for some years. It was very difficult and tiresome. I had to leave work on several occasions and stay up many late nights. I don't remember her father ever going to the Dr with me, strange.

After some time had passed we decided we wanted to buy a house, I wanted out of the relationship but did not want to go back to my mother's. I felt so stuck, I was only making enough money to pay the bills, so I thought, although my boyfriend was bringing home his paycheck. I was thinking I needed bigger bucks. It never dawned on me to put away even small amounts if that is all I had.

We bought a VA house a fixer upper, porch house 3 bedroom hardwood floors after we stripped up the green dirty cat smelling carpet. Our mortgage was under $400 a month. Great deal.

The emotional abuse never stopped with him criticizing me and putting me down and comparing me to his ex girlfriends. He kept drinking his Jack Daniel's and now he was doing drugs. He was beginning to run in and out of the house at strange times of the night. He would ask me for money saying that he owed it to someone that would hurt him. I always had this fear about drug addicts and drug dealers, I knew I had to find away out.

I was pregnant again. By this time I was depressed something had to change. I was working late as possible; I was staying up late nights waiting for him to get to sleep so I could just crawl into bed. Reality had smacked me in my face. I had finally come to the realization that this man was afraid to get married and was not going to change. He told me that marriage was too permanent.

I spent seven years of my life with a man that thinks marriage is too permanent. He also acted as if he was afraid to tell me that he loved me. It was like getting a tooth pulled for him. Probably issues from the past two ex's. ***Momma said, "Never feel sorry for a man he may not be looking for a wife, he may be content shacking up with you."***

I had another beautiful little girl. I worked until the day I had her. I was exhausted. Then six months after I gave birth, I finally developed the faith to leave. I was watching a lot of Christian television during this time. I packed what I could carry with the two girls and walked to the subway. I pretended I was going out for a while. During this time, his brother came to visit, he was watching me strangely.

I started walking for the train and here comes my children's father down the subway steps. He began to question me and threaten me. I was so afraid but I refused to go back. I just waited for the train, he did not want to get locked up I guess, so he left.

By this time my mother was living some place else, much better living conditions then our old condemned house, but a small rental. I asked if I could stay, she let me stay for a night, and then complained about her landlord situation. She insisted that I go back to my house and baby daddy. She stated she would never leave her house. I was disappointed, I really wanted her to understand what I had been through.

The house and the new furniture was not worth my sanity and my girls seeing me abused. I went back for one day, and decided it was a mistake. I felt more sorry for myself and little girls than for him. He blocked me on the stairway, and threatened me. He said "If you were not a Christian I would hurt you". I left again and never went back.

**Momma said, "never feel sorry for a man". That is how it all began, of course I did not listen when she tried to warn me."**

It was a difficult time. My brother remembered the time I helped him when he wanted to finish school. He had a small apartment in South Philly. He told me to bring the girls and come with him. We stayed in a small room with a small crib and twin bed. My daughter and I shared the bed, by now she was maybe four years old. I was so stressed, I had very little money, my job was being phased out and my hours was cut. I worked temp jobs for some time while looking for another permanent job. I caught the bus to drop the girls to my sister's house in North Philly while I worked, then my oldest started Kindergarten.

I was very lonely and feeling as if things were hopeless. I had joined a church in Germantown, where a co worker I believed worshipped. They really took to me and my daughters. They would send the van to pick us up from South Philly and take us to Germantown and then back home again. I was grateful.

It was still a stressful life. I wanted my own again. At some point I had to apply for public assistance. While attending church I learned the principle of tithing. I decided I would tithe no matter what, and I did even if we were low on food. I lost some weight, although I thought my face was too pointy. I made sure the girls ate even if I had a little.

# Chapter 3

## Out of the frying pan into the fire

*Remember Anita Baker's song "Rapture" ? I was hooked on the whole cd and living in a fantasy world.*

My brother was working in the evenings. One beautiful Spring day, in 1986, after church I took the girls and went to my friend Lisa's house to see she and her mother. Her mother was like a grandmother to me. I needed the support. It was a Memorial Day holiday weekend. She loved to cook and she had invited us over. After I left her home I was waiting for the bus at 29th and Girard Ave. I had some religious tracts with me and was giving them out to people who were at the bus stop. There stood a nice looking guy with a Budweiser beer in his hand with shiny baby skin and nice looking brown complexion. I wasn't checking him, altho it seemed like I was the way I just described him. But later realized that he was checking me.

He liked my black skirt set with New York buildings painted all over them in white. I had my little one in the stroller and I was holding the hand of the oldest one. Then we started talking after he complimented my outfit. I gave him a tract. The bus was taking long probably because it was a Sunday. Anyway, it finally came I thanked him for helping me put the stroller on the bus. Then he decided to sit with us. He appeared to be going all the way my way, like South Philly. This was six months after I had left my children's father. **Momma said, "never feel sorry for a man, you may give him a tract and not be able to get rid of him, or you may want to redeem him."**

He followed me off of the bus, I was a little nervous about that. We sat on my steps and talked for hours. I put the kids in bed came back outside and we talked some more. He was someone I could connect with and someone else to feel sorry for. He appeared to be secretive and I did not see that as a signal to get out quickly.

Someone was paying me attention again. He grew up in North Philly had a hard childhood just like me. His father was a alcoholic and he always felt abandoned by his mother, we have a lot in common. He had anger issues towards his parents that should have been a red flag but it wasn't. I was too wounded myself. This night started another cycle of dysfunction. **Momma said, "Never feel sorry for a man." It could be the beginning of a crazy cycle."**

My brother started a new relationship, and he decided to move her and her son in with us. Things got worse as his girlfriend clearly showed us in her own way that she did not want us there. I thought I was doing the best I could at the time. The guy I met, we were seeing each other for some time, we hung out with the kids, sometimes I took them to my mother's or sister's and we would just walk and talk. Then we decided we were going to do it, you know what I mean. I had backslid out of loneliness and self-pity. Actually I wanted to be rescued. Had my knight in shining armor really showed up? I did not want to get pregnant so we went to Rite Aide and got some contraceptives. Of course we went back and did it. I later realized I was pregnant because what I had purchased, I was suppose to use more than once after a certain time frame during intercourse. I told him that I was pregnant, he thought that I had set him up and chose to disappear for a few months. I was devastated and could not understand why this would happen to me. Could it have been because I was not making good choices?

I felt God was mad at me for being so weak and foolish. I had major issues, although at this time I did not know what issues was. He showed up eventually, of course I forgave him because I made a promise to myself that I would not be alone with another child and this was my second baby daddy. I **had** to make this work. **Says who?** God laughs at our plans . . . remember?

One night we were invited to a small house party in North Philly. I took the children to my mother's house. I met up with him. We went to the party and his friends were not really my type of friends although I tried to fit in. I think I had a drink not much and he was drinking a lot, shot after shot. He appeared to be showing off for his friends. At some point, he pulled down his pants showing his bare butt. I was embarrassed and I told him that he was embarrassing me and to stop it.

I decided I was going to leave. I started walking down the stairs and then down the street. I heard glass breaking, he had thrown his drink at me. I had a strange feeling in my stomach about this night. Although, I wanted to take off and run I didn't. I knew he would probably catch me. I watched as he walked closer to me, I was not sure what he was going to do.

I wondered if any of his friends who had left the party had been watching us and would try to calm him down. They didn't. Nobody wanted to get involved, actually I believe that they were afraid of him, I was too. We were in the area where most of his family lived near Cecil B Moore.

Although I had lived in the area during those traumatic days when I was a little girl, I still felt alone and far away from home.

He walked toward me; I backed up against the concrete wall. He looked at me and said, "I should bash your head against that wall". I wondered what I had done so wrong to deserve that. I did not want to imagine my brains on that wall. He did not do it, I started walking up the street, some how we ended up walking down a smaller street. It was also a darker street. No one was around.

He once again started to threaten me. It was close to 2 a.m. The night felt scary, as if demons were lurking around us. I saw some people coming out of a bar that seemed to be closing and asked for their help in a calm way. I really wanted to scream, "help me!!" He heard me and pulled me away. We began to walk closer to Ridge Ave and I saw a taxi. I took a chance and flagged it down, I just wanted to get back to my mother's house and my children. I wondered if I would see them again.

I flagged down the taxi and jumped in trying to quickly close the door so he would not get in. He grabbed my handbag and we both were pulling it back and forth. He won the tug of war and jumped in the taxi with me. I wanted the taxi to take me to my mother's but he told the taxi to take us to South Philly, that is where I was staying at the time, with my brother. The taxi driver seemed afraid of him, and actually accepted the $5 that he was only willing to pay for such a long trip.

There was a silent rage in him. I wanted him to calm down, we talked and went back to my brother's place and eventually went to sleep. We got up the next morning as if nothing never happened holding hands etc. He appeared to be really sorry for his behavior, apologizing. We rode the bus together back to North Philly to get the children. I was so happy to see my two girls. I was pregnant with the third one, his child.

He would come and go and decided to stay away for the remainder of my pregnancy. He would call every few days and I would just wait for the call like a wounded bird looking for her mother or father.

I had a great-aunt who lived near by and would help me from time to time even if my money ran low. I kept my man problems away from her. I was ashamed. I don't know why, all of her men were alcoholics. She must have been feeling sorry for them too. I could never understand how she could even kiss these nasty men with such horrible teeth in their mouths. I guess it was the money. She probably wanted it for her gambling habit and recent trips to Atlantic City.

I had stopped going to the church in Germantown, I was so ashamed and embarrassed by my choices. I remember the Pastor begging me not to leave or keep seeing this man. It was too late I was PREGNANT. I had to handle this problem myself. I never thought about staying in church and allowing God to help me work it out. I did not know Faith was a action word.

A few months had passed. I went to visit my friend whom I had been friends with since my early teens. She lived in South Philly not too far away from where I was staying. I went to visit her, I knew that I was in labor. When I got to her house I told her that I was going to have the baby tonight. She was surprised that I thought I was such a pro after only having two children.

Her son and boyfriend was home, we decided to go in the other room and talk for privacy. Then we all watched TV for a while. She and I talked and talked. The pains began to get worse, I decided to go home in a taxi. I was tired by this time and just wanted to sleep. I got to my brother's apartment and decided I would lay down. Now the pains felt like somebody with a size 12 was trying to crush my back. I did not feel like a pro now. I decided to wake up my brother, we got the children and he called my mother.

I remember getting in his small blue station wagon in so much pain. He looked nervous and I just wanted the baby to come out but not in the station wagon. We got to the hospital and I asked the Dr to give me some pain medicine. He said it was too late, I was nine centimeters. The so called pro almost had the baby in her brother's apartment. I had no choice. I was going to have this baby without anesthesia.

Oh, well. the hospital was nice and cozy. I had a very nurturing nurse. At this time it was very important for me because I was tired and felt very alone because the father of my child had abandoned me. He thought that I had tricked him because the birth control was used incorrectly. ***Mamma said, "never feel sorry for a man". I did and I was rejected and abandoned."***

I should have left him on that corner that Spring evening and never said anything to him. I could have given him a religious tract and got on the bus and ignored him. Or when he got off the bus with me I could have said something to drive him away, so that he could not see where I lived. He would have gone to see the girl that he was suppose to be going to see around the corner, but instead got off of the bus with me. Yea right, lucky me huh?

My brother went to get my mother and she was also a great support system. She stayed during the remainder of my delivery and it went well. One and a half hour later I gave birth to a beautiful little girl that looked like someone else gave birth to her. She was beautiful and chocolate brown, she looked just like her father.

My mother and I looked at her and we both just broke out laughing, cause I am red bone tone. We both knew that he could not deny this child if he tried. She had long hair all down her neck and I was not angry with her. I loved this baby. Actually I felt compassion for her because I knew that her father probably not be there for her. She would feel abandoned by her father just like I did. He called on the phone the next day, and when he found out that I had given birth to a girl, he said, "you can't have any boys"? What a jerk. I should have named my book, never feel sorry for a jerk.

Later, after I returned home, I use to look in her bassinet and cry and apologize to her, because he was not there. In many ways he did deny her. I loved playing peek a boo with her in the bassinet. Her mouth would open so wide. She surly had his mouth. I would laugh at that time, although I didn't laugh much during those days. **Momma said, "never feel sorry for a man, you might lose your joy".**

I finally got tired of waiting and out of anger I decided to take our baby and go to his father's home in North Philly. I would ask his sister's if he was around. If he was not around, I would sit there with her hoping that he would show up. Sometimes he would show up and sometimes he wouldn't. At this time I did not know that my behavior was controlling and needy. But remember I HAD to make this work, he was my second baby daddy. What would people think of me? My childhood dream of being married and having two children had already been off track.

I had gone to looking for him more than once, this went on for some time. We eventually started seeing each other again. *I always fell for the apologies. Momma said, "never feel sorry for a man".*

I was on a mission to make my life work the best way I knew how. I manipulated, I controlled, I screamed, I criticized, I compromised. I was looking for love in a man that did not know how to love me. I did not love myself. We made a nice couple. Yea right!

We finally moved in together, of course I got the house, then he moved in. I worked, I paid the bills I took the kids to preschool and he did what he knew how to do best. He did, Street. He decided to become a lookout for the drug dealers. Who created that job description? He would sit on the corner late hours of the night talk and drink beer. *Momma said, "never feel sorry for a man" He may not want a REAL job, he may not work at all."*

Me, being a caretaker, my mother had left her boyfriend and was living with me, my sister who kept running out of the bathroom naked because her room was next to the bathroom was living with me. My brother who was indecisive about helping with the bills was living with me. My mother's husband, whom she had been separated from for years was now living in my basement with her. How did I get in this mess? *Never feel sorry for people, compassion is one thing, helping is another, but enabling is unacceptable."*

One night, my brother's girlfriend gave a birthday party at my house. I never went anywhere, because I was depending on my boyfriend to take me. If he didn't then I did not go. Of, course I could not go out alone or with a friend. Insanity. Anyway, I wanted to look really nice, my hair was long and I was proud of it, so I got it done. I went and bought a nice dress, everyone was looking nice. My mother and brothers and sisters were there with a few friends and neighbors. I wanted to look nice for DC. He looked at me, and seemed to be insecure.

My brother was with two of his friends and I was told by DC that one of my brother's friends was eyeing me. I honestly had not noticed. I only had eyes for DC. Everything was peaceful, until my youngest brother and I got into an argument about a cassette tape he had borrowed from me. After having too many drinks, he lunged at me and DC was on his throat and they both came crashing down on top of the table. People at the party broke it up. I knew it was too good to be true, drama.

Well, after the party, DC kept bringing up this guy, who I didn't even remember. Mostly every one had left, it was quiet and probably after 2 a.m. My mother and her boyfriend, because the husband thing didn't last long, went for a walk. In other words the husband moved out after she discovered that he was shooting heroine in his feet and groin. He had been on drugs for years, that and his cheating was the main reason they had split. He never hit her. I could give him credit for that.

I was living in North Philly near 4th and Lehigh, drugs and totally ghetto neighborhood; not a good place to raise your three girls, but affordable for the year and a half that I lived there. As we were walking, I began to feel DC slowing down as if he wanted them to walk further ahead.

My stomach began to get that sinking feeling, like that night of his friend's party. I did not understand his behavior. He was accusing me over and over again about my brother's friend, whom till this day I do not remember. He started to pull on me, I was wondering if he was going to hit me or something with my mother and her boyfriend just a few feet away. Insane. **Momma said, "never feel sorry for a man he may be jealous and very insecure."**

I started walking ahead so I could get closer to my mother. If he would have hit me, my mother would have gone insane. She has never allowed anyone to put her hands on us. Even during the times when we were little and she was being abused, she would never let those men touch her children. I thank God for that. She would fight back the best she knew how. She would find a way sometimes to get revenge, such as waiting until he went to sleep and bash him in the eyes with the tip of the iron. He would wake up with two black eyes closed shut. Insane. I was about ten years old then. **Momma said, "Never feel sorry for a man; You may see him get abused." The tables sometimes turn.**

Once I got closer to my mother and her boyfriend, he seemed to catch himself. I was grateful another fight did not break out. It was a difficult relationship yet I refused to let go. I had many reasons to let go, but I guess I was afraid of being alone with the children. Why did I think I was safe with him was insane.

He would stay out late, and hang in the bars. I would go around the corner to his aunt's house and gripe and complain. It felt so good to have someone listen to me and actually take my side. She would cuss him out whenever she would see him. Of course, that only made him angry. I felt like a victim, I did not realize I had choices, and confiding in her would only make things worse. "**Momma said, never feel sorry for a man he may become even more rebellious.**"

I just wanted someone to listening ear. I am sure he saw it as control and manipulation. I am sure that is exactly what it turned into. I was young soul sick and did not understand my own dysfunction. *Momma said" Never feel sorry for a man".*

He will stay out late and party with other women and will not take you anywhere. He will abuse you and disrespect you and then apologize and start all over again. Insanity is doing the same thing over and over again and expecting different results.

I decided to take a class cause it was taking too long to get another job after I was laid off. It took nine months to finish my class. I was never one to sit around, at least for long. I left a job here and there to be with my girls, especially if the money was not good. I finished my class with excellent grades.

As I was sending off resumes to find another job, I decided to visit the school and practice to keep up my skills. I saw a job opportunity at Amtrak. I decided to take the test. I was worried but, I passed the test with flying colors and was called for an interview. Someday, because of this job my life would change, but I did not know it at this time. It was divine intervention. I later found out that Amtrak rarely hire people from the outside because the employees usually bid on the jobs.

I went to the interview and believe it or not although the money was good, I was not excited about the job when I realized I would be working in a department with several employees. I had worked in this type of environment during my late teens and early twenties. There was a bad taste in my mouth. I am not stupid I was offered the job and took it.

I was an excellent employee with superior ratings during evaluation time. I was proud of myself. I did not pat myself on the back often. But was grateful for the job. I made new friends and learned how to set boundaries in my relationships. My last department job, things got out of control, with people being in my personal business.

Home was not a happy place for me. When I would get home from work, because DC worked at night as a lookout, he would spend a lot of time in bed, and of course I would find myself just hanging out in the room with him. That was the only privacy we had, since so many of my relatives was living with us.

# Chapter 4

## *New Home . . . New Season*

Some time later I received a letter in the mail. After applying for public housing over four years ago, I had finally gotten an offer. I was in shock and so excited. I knew deep within me I really needed a change. I began to set some boundaries, although I did not know what I was doing was called setting boundaries. I told everyone in the house that my girls and I were moving and they could not come with us. Momma was not happy, she wanted me to feel sorry for my baby sister and her son at least take them with me. My mind was made up, everyone was adults. I felt that if I could make it with three little girls, then she could take care of her son. It took nine months for the renovations to be completed but then I was in.

I made another good choice, I told DC that he could not come if he did not make an effort to change. That is exactly what he did, made an effort. At some point I started going back to church, so he decided one night he would go with me to bible study. He seemed to like Rev. Rice. and he decided to receive Christ as His Lord and Savior. That did not last long, just long enough for him to get in the new bi-level apartment with me and the kids. He went back to his normal routine. Actually, he got worse. **Momma said, "never feel** *sorry for a man" he will do just about anything to get his way and he will tell a woman just what she wants to hear."*

Anyway, we had been together maybe 5 years by this time. The next 4 years would be harder to handle. He would stay out all night, sometimes 2 nights. He would come home and ask me what was for dinner? He would even bring change of clothes home smelling Downy fresh. I would yell and sometimes he would shut down and retreat to the room. He would stay there for a day or two and then back off to the streets.

I got pregnant again, we decided we would get married. It probably was me controlling because here comes child number four. We went to get the license and the blood test. By the time we arrived home he had changed into a raging man. I did not understand. My emotions were like the sea, powerful. They were hard to feel so my body would go back into trauma mode. I would shut down and go numb.

He retreated to the bedroom, and shut down. He lay in the dark, maybe grieving the life he did not want to give up. I tried to talk to him and get him to open up to me but he just looked at me as if he wanted to hurt me. I knew to get out of the bedroom. *Momma said, "never feel sorry for a man". He may decide one minute he will marry you and then turn into Dr. Jekyl.*

# Chapter 5

## *Rehab? Not Me!!*

I went into the bathroom devastated as if I was left at the alter. I was sick and tired of being sick and tired. My thinking was distorted, meaning I was not myself. I wanted to hurt him, I was tired of trying to make everything work. I went into my little half bath and cried out to God for help. I said, ""God there has to be more to life than this, please show me". And He did. I was where he needed me to be. Surrendered.

I went to work the next day, depressed and tired and shut down. I sat at my desk. I worked in the Revenue Department on the 4th floor. Anyway, we had good benefits and the money was good. God had set me up. Amtrak had an EAP(Employee Assistance Program). It was there for employees that were going through difficulties, addictive behaviors, depression or those who needed Counseling. **"Momma said" never feel sorry for a man you may suffer with depression."**

I realized that some of my co-workers were leaving for a month or so and coming back refreshed in good spirits. I also knew they were going to places like Florida. Tears streamed down my face and

I got up from my desk and went to the EAP Department. I spoke to the EAP representative and told him that I needed to get away.

At the time I was in denial about where I would be going. I suggested Florida, and they said that the rules had been changed and I could not go. I was so disappointed. I was also told if I had a relative's address that I could use, they could make it happen.

My aunt that was in South Philly with me way back when had moved to Virginia. I gave them her address. I was told that I could go to Florida. I contacted my mother and sister whom I had left in the house in Philly. I told them that I was going away, and needed someone to watch the children for 2 weeks.

While DC was out doing his thing I was making plans. I guess he did not take me serious either. The people that I helped was not there for me at least at that time. They were angry cause I would not let them move into the new bi-level apt with us.

I called my aunt who was in VA. I asked her could she watch the children for two weeks. I told her that my job was sending me somewhere. She thought it was a business trip and agreed to watch them.

I went home and told my children; they did not understand. My oldest daughter was maybe 9 at the time. She had gotten use to hiding her feelings. My heart really went out to my girls. But I knew it was something I had to do, I felt like I was losing it. I did it for them not just myself. My children meant the world to me.

Since I worked for Amtrak I also had train benefits. I packed up the children and myself and we headed for the train station and then Virginia. My aunt was very understanding. The children were very sad and so was I. My oldest daughter went into the bathroom and came out. I could tell she had been crying.

I had a flight almost immediately to Tampa Bay Florida. I had never flown before. It started to rain, for me that made things worse. I walked away from my children at that apartment building as they all stood outside with my aunt. It was a step of faith that I would not regret. But at the time, I wondered if I would see my children again. I still get a little emotional when I think about that day in Aug of 1992.

I arrived at the airport, I prayed every chance I got for God to give me strength. I was very fearful and full of anxiety. I arrived on the plane and sat down. I believe that God sent me two angels on this trip. The first one was sitting next to me. He had a friendly face and was dressed professionally.

He was a tall white man in uniform, and some how we started talking, and I am sure I told him that I had never flown before. He was compassionate towards me and told me that he flew all the time. He said all the right things. I began to relax at some point I was beginning to feel safe.

But then there was a problem with the plane, something was broken and it was a storm and the plane could not navigate through the storm without it. We had to land in West Palm Beach. I looked for him when I got off of the plan but he seemed to have disappeared.

I felt lost and anxiety was beginning to return then I believe my second angel showed up. A white man seemed to almost stop just for me when I arrived in the airport. He practically told me where to go before I could finish telling him what I needed to do. I felt more confident as he walked away. I knew God was with me.

I called my mother just to hear someones voice that sounded familiar. I needed to not feel alone. She was supportive although I am sure she did not know what was really going on. We did not have to wait too long in West Palm Beach. We boarded on another plane and about an hour later we were landing in Tampa Bay Florida. I was so grateful to have made it that far.

We landed maybe after 9p.m. When I got off of the plane, a man was waiting for me with my name on a piece of paper. That was strange to me, but things was going as planned. We boarded a van and I watched as buildings and trees and houses passed me by. I like scenery but it was hard to see in the dark. I wished it was a sunny day.

Then maybe less than an hour, I arrived at a one story building, nice modern design. It was called the Care Unit. I went inside, it was spacious, and had a lot of windows for natural light. I love natural lighting although it was still night time. I was greeted by a women who took my vital signs and a urine specimen.

Then another woman showed up and the women that greeted me told her that I was not an addict but Codependent. I asked her what was Codependent, and she told me that I would find out. I felt as if I was in a small hospital but I was not confined to my bed. Strangely I felt I was in the right place.

I was taken to my room, I felt so numb and isolated and sometimes I would feel anxious and afraid. I knew in my heart that God had led me to this place but I did not have all the answers. I was challenged to trust Him. I asked God was I suppose to be in this place. I knew deep inside me that He said yes and to Trust Him. I had come this far, on a plane alone and my children in VA. Why not trust God now. I was not doing it before. Instead I was trying to control everything in my life.

I was given a schedule of things to do the next day. A day in rehab began early I mean like 6 a.m. what a change. First we got up and went into the gym and laid on some mats. There was an instructor.

But we were not exercising we were learning how to relax and meditate. There was music relaxing music playing. We had to close our eyes and force ourselves to relax and picture the ocean or some place relaxing. I guess it was my first lesson in being in the moment. We also recited the Lord's Prayer. Matthew 6:9-13

This was different, I kinda wandered around just doing as I was told for almost two weeks before I got to a real place of acceptance and confidence. I told my aunt I would be gone for two weeks. When in reality I did not want to accept that I would actually be gone for twenty eight days. I was afraid to leave the kids that long. But again I needed to trust God and let go of the fear and the need to control.

I realized what they were showing me at this place was good. The bible says: **My people perish for lack of knowledge. Hosea 4:6** After meditation we would eat breakfast and off to some lecture. I learned about drugs and alcohol and most of *all* **addictive behaviors** sometimes we were formed in a group. Group was really intense and emotional at times.

People had all kinds of issues from their past to deal with. There was a young man who had never grieved the death of his father. The Therapist in the group set him up by giving him the opportunity to do it. They used a role play method. I watched as the Therapist would target different individuals in the group.

Then one day my turn came. I was so confidently walking around the place dressed in all black in denial about my feelings and the pain I held deep inside. I had been used, abused, victimized and always portrayed the image as if I had it all together. I was a survivor. I was still here.

I liked telling others what to do and giving them advice. That allowed me to take my mind off of my crazy life, meaning whatever dysfunctional relationship I was in at the time. Strangely, I can talk about it now. The Therapist began to ask me how I felt, and of course I answered as if I was great. In reality, he knew that I was not great. Actually I didn't know how I felt, numb.

He started saying things to embarrass me, he was reading me and he was doing it well. He went into my past and bought up people that hurt me. I felt like he was attacking me. His goal was to help me break out of the denial and get in touch with my feelings. I know this now but at the time I did not know. People were watching and I wondered what they thought of me.

I fell apart, I cried and sat in the corner like a baby, asking why did he do this and that to me, asking why did people hurt me? I was scarred emotionally and physically. I was use to the fear and that kept me in survival mode most days. I knew I had to survive. The Therapist said I was suicidal and homicidal. Yeah right, probably more homicidal than suicidal. Suicidal by not taking care of myself I guess, and taking care of everyone else. ***"Momma said, never feel sorry for a man, you may not know who you are."***

One of the Therapist's name was Jay he was a tall white man who wore cow boy boots, had long hair and a beard. Sometimes him and Kathleen would work together as a team. They were excellent at helping us emotionally soul sick people. Actually, they shared their stories with us. They use to be us.

I knew Jay knew what he was talking about, when he said that I was homicidal. If felt scary though. Why? Because, that is one of the reasons why I went to my job for help. My thinking was not right, I wanted to seriously hurt my husband. I knew it was time to get help.

I was a God fearing person who knew better than that. In spite of my hurt, I knew I was a good person. Why did I love this type of man? ***Momma said "never feel sorry for a man, you may get angry enough to want to hurt him."***

Back at home, my children's father was angry and acting out and decided to send my mother to get the children from my aunt's place in Virginia. Oh, boy, I was not happy about that. I was allowed to call home at some point, he would throw down the phone and break it. He was not happy, because I kept telling him that I wanted to break up with him. I feared going home and facing him in my life again. My family thought I was crazy I guess, but the good thing was they helped him with the children, as crazy as it seems he took good care of them for the remainder of my 28 day stay at the Care Unit.

I loved that name, The Care Unit, they took good care of me. I was use to caring for others. I was learning how to love me and give myself permission to live. It felt scary, I was anxious most of the time. Most people there were not only Codependent but drug addicts and alcoholics as well. I enjoyed going to group and the chemical addiction workshops.

I always did love knowledge and classroom settings. The Professors were understanding and very knowledgeable. We learned all about addictive behaviors including being addicted to people, places, and things. This addiction stuff is huge and also destroying millions of people's lives. The bible says that we must renew our minds.

I was slowly learning new ways to cope and take care of myself. Although I did not know what a healthy relationship was. We were taken to meetings, AA and Coda and whatever meetings they took us to including NA meetings. The principles were all the same so were the 12 steps. The 12 steps are 12 principles that help a person soul sick like me at the time, to find herself and her Higher Power (God). "Jesus is my Lord & Savior."

Actually, they were like a compass that led me to a relationship with God, self and others. My self esteem was so warped I did not have a clue that God cared for me. I always felt he was angry with me. I guess I forgot He sent His son to die for me on the cross. My thinking was more religious. I did not know much about God's grace and mercy.

Working the 12 principles helped me realize that God loves me and was not angry with me. I did not know that God wanted to help me. I always felt that I was not good enough and still sometimes struggle with old stinking thinking. He cares about all of His creation.

While I was at the Care Unit I connected with some people, one young man seemed to be obsessed with me and what I was doing. That is so Codependent. His name was Sid. He was constantly on my back because he felt that I was making friends with the wrong people, particularly a guy.

Old behaviors don't vanish overnight, it takes a lot of practice. Actually, he was right I had become buddies with an addict, not a good choice. But in reality he needed to focus on his own recovery not mine. It got so bad that Sid was stalking me and insulting me.

One day I got tired of him stalking me and we had a heated argument. I began to charge at him, and the others had to pull us apart so we would not fight. He only added to my anxiety. I had been nice to him at some point. I believe he had a crush on me, he looked like a psycho to me, somebody from a "LifeTime" movie. Not my type, thick glasses, chubby and kinda weird. **Momma said "Never feel sorry for a man he might stalk you. Insane I know."**

I met Jackie a young black light skinned lady also an addict with freckles. We would go to group together, we were also roommates.

She had so many problems just like me. But she also had so many strengths, just like me. I was voted President of the Group and Jackie was voted Vice President.

It was something they did every few weeks I believe. We were a team, we helped make decisions for the group and called to order the group meetings. The members of the group would share their feelings about whatever was on their minds. In this group we learned how to value our feelings.

I learned some good things about myself at the Care Unit. I learned I had leadership skills and good influence over others. People saw me as a good person. We made tee shirts and those in the group had to put words on it to affirm the good they saw in us. My shirt said all these nice things about me, funny I was usually to busy condemning myself to see what others saw.

Although, strangely when someone hurt me, I acted as if I was this perfect person. I would go from self-righteous to arrogant to being a victim in a short period of time. I was a messed up young women who felt like a little girl inside still wanting her daddy to come and rescue her. I was living in my past wanting to get free but didn't know how. I wanted to know what love really felt like. But at the same time could not recognize it.

I was a mother of three precious little girls. I was not there for them emotionally but allowed them to be there for each other. I clothed them and cooked for them but it was always about the responsibility and not the joy of being a mother.

I regretted not playing with them and laughing with them enough. I did enjoy taking them places to play. I did the best I knew how to do at the time with what I knew. I did not give myself permission to have fun, I felt I did not have time, I had to take care of my children.

I forget how I use to laugh and joke around with family and friends. Life was serious.

The 28 days was going fast and I was not ready to go home. One person in the group had who had never grieved his relative's death was being targeted. Jay and Kathleen had it all planned. We were told to be quiet. We sat with the lights dimmed, and they called on the person.

Someone was lying on the floor covered with a sheet as this person was told to say his or her goodbyes to the relative. It was a sad moment, but the person got a breakthrough. I was fascinated with recovery and the new tools, the books, everything. I wanted to become a Counselor or help in someway of course when I got more practice and my own breakthroughs.

I wanted to go home and tell the world all about recovery. I was a little upset that I did not know that it even existed. *I didn't know that I could change my way of thinking and change my life. I did not know that I had choices.* I grew up believing you were stuck with whatever life dealt you. My eyes were opening up but I had more healing to do a lot more. I had a lot more tears to shed and mistakes to make.

# Chapter 6

## *Going Home Façing Reality*

It was time to go home, I barely remember the flight. I know I prayed because I was so anxious. I was glad to see my children and wondering if I could be a better mother a better person. I was sent home on anti-depressants which I was not happy about. I was afraid of becoming addicted. I accepted the fact that they were helping me for a time. But eventually, I weened myself off of them.

My job also paid for a Psychiatrist, after a few weeks he sent me off to heal. My baby's daddy, was still doing what he wanted to do. I got tired, started crying less and going to Ala-non meetings. This is a support group for family members and friends of Alcoholics. (well my boyfriend had a drinking problem, dad was an alcoholic and my mom's crazy boyfriends were heavy drinkers). Looks like I qualify for help. I had been affected by someone else's drinking.

I was working my recovery, and focusing more on me then on him and what he was doing. I made new friends in recovery; I went to all types of meetings and started doing service. It was a way to get involved and out of my own head. That is when you start helping out at the meetings and chairing meetings as well. Some day, I may help other people in recovery.

I wanted to be a drug and alcohol counselor, so I thought. I figured although I could not help my boyfriend I could help those who wanted help. I was happier than ever. ***Not because he had changed but because I had changed.*** I was no longer depending on him or some one else for my happiness. Taking responsibility for my choices felt good. I was working what I learned, but not perfectly.

I got pregnant again and was not happy about it at first. I had three beautiful girls already but I always wanted a son. Maybe this time it would be a boy. I was good at rationalizing. I made a promise to myself when I was younger to never have another abortion if I was old enough to take care of the baby. I would trust God to provide. Besides I believe that I have two babies already waiting for me when I get to Heaven.

I was gaining weight. I hated gaining weight. Why did I have to go around this mountain again? Or was it the same mountain? Actually, it was a continuation of a journey that I was on. Recovery is a life long process of up the mountain and down the mountain. Believe it or not it got crazy. What was I thinking? Well of course, I was not where I wanted to be emotionally or spiritually, but I guess I was where I needed to be in order to get the lesson. ***Momma said" never feel sorry for a man you may feel as if you are going backwards".***

I was pregnant; now what am I going to do? Boy it's easy to get in, but not as easy to get out. I knew he was not healthy for me to be with, meaning his character had not changed. Of course he made some changes but it did not take long before he returned to old behaviors such as staying out all night, well actually now he was staying out one night instead of two. And sometimes he would actually come in around 3 am. that was progress to him. ***Momma*** said *"never feel sorry for a man"* *he might go back to old behaviors."*

During my pregnancy he was not available most times; I usually felt abandoned by him. This was one reason why I did not want another baby. Strangely, I got pregnant worrying about smoking and birth control pills and the side affects from that(blood clots). I got pregnant changing birth control methods so I could still smoke. Insanity, I know. I decided to stop smoking after being pregnant a few months. I did not want to hurt the baby, *funny I was able to do it for the baby but not for myself . . . . hmmmm.* **Think.**

D.C. would come home and isolate for a few days and then hit the streets again. I would leave his dinner in the microwave and go to bed. This was progress for me; there were times when I would stay up late and look out of the third floor window to see if his truck was pulling up.

One night to my surprise, the truck went by the house quickly, I know I saw a person next to him that looked like a woman with a big afro. Of course, later when I confronted him, he did not know what I was talking about. He never admitted doing anything. After some investigating, I found out that the hair belonged to a sister of a friend of his. From time to time he would just look at me and say, **"for what it's worth**, I do love you."

It didn't mean much to me, there was so much disappointment in the relationship. I realized that he loved me the best way he knew how. But it was not the love that I needed. *I had settled for a love that was not of God.* He was a man that did not love himself; I did not love myself, and did not want to be single with children. *Momma said, "never feel sorry for a man you may be lonely feel stuck with a lot of regrets."*

# Chapter 7

## Yes . . . I Married Him

We found out this baby would be a boy, and as crazy as it may seem, we decided to get married. Insanity had showed it's ugly face again. I had reasoned myself into another bad choice. We decided to get the blood test taken. After—wards he began to act strange, distant and a silent rage came over him.

We arrived home and he went up to the bedroom. I stayed downstairs trying to sort things out in my head about his behavior. I knew deep in my soul that he knew marriage would intrude on his freedom. I decided to go upstairs to see how he was feeling. The room was dark, It felt as if I had entered the room with a demon. I could feel the anger in the darkness, sort of like the calm before the storm.

I asked if he was alright. His voice changed; it grew deeper. He told me to get out. I left the room quickly, telling myself that he was very angry and needed some space. Although, I could feel this sinking feeling in my stomach. *Fear and self-pity came over me like a flood.* I took his behavior very personally. **Momma said, "never**

**feel sorry for a man he may turn into Dr. Jeykl if he does not want to commit." "He may be afraid of change."**

At some point he snapped out of it and we decided to set a date. I told my sister that I was getting married in August and she was upset because she was planning to get married I believe in October. Now I was going through drama with my sister. I did not understand her behavior.

I was getting married at the justice of the peace and she was having a real wedding with a dress, bridesmaids the works. I suggested a double wedding, but how dare me even think of something like that at least in her mind. Well although some sisters have done it, it was not her choice.

I was four months pregnant and did not want this baby to come into the world without me being married. It was all apart of me still trying to make my fantasy come true. I had three children already with two different last names. "What would other people think of me, and I was not married yet?" I decided to go and get married without my family. I was ashamed anyway, everyone knew of my dysfunctional relationship. My family did not understand what I saw in him, "he is a street guy my sister use to say." Never-mind she was with a street guy too. It's so easy for us to focus on other peoples' relationships so we won't have to focus on the insanity that is in ours. *Denial is not a river in Egypt.*

He did not have a suit, so he wore his black short set and sandals. I wore a suit, cream skirt and green jacket with tiny flowers. It was all I had to wear. I really wished that we had the money for a wedding dress and a suit for him. My dream wedding was only a fantasy. It was a nice place and we took pictures in the courtyard. The girls were young and did not understand, but we had said our vows promising to love each other till death do us part. ***Momma*** said" "never feel sorry for a man, you may be too ashamed to invite your family to the ceremony."

I loved my children so much, and wanted to be the best mom ever. But of course, I made some bad choices along the way. I did not set an example with for my children. *I did the best I could with what I knew.* I was not a liar but I was good at lying to myself by rationalizing many of my decisions. My innocent children were caught in the insanity of this codependent marriage. *They loved him; he was their daddy. I guess the girls were happy to have some kind of daddy in their life. I felt sorry for myself and them too. I even felt sorry for him sometimes.* **"Momma said" "never feel sorry for a man you may become his number one enabler."**

After we got married, I went back to work, at Amtrak. I received a strange call from a woman named Sandra. My husband knew her before me. She was a bit older and had a little girl by him before we met. She also had several other children. I was shocked that she called my job and could not figure out how she got the phone number to the department I was in. She claimed she called just to inform me that she was out of the picture for good and that she was not an adulterer. It really sent her for a loop that he had married me and not her. **"Momma said" "never feel sorry for a man, he may have some unfinished business with other women."**

The so called woman that was not an adulterer, seemed to call the house on a regular basis and hang up after we got married. Sometimes she would call me a b——h and hang up. I would confront my husband about his so called ex. He would never admit he was still seeing her. Although one night while we were in bed, he slipped and called me Sannie. Of course, when I asked him did he call me Sannie, he denied it.

I could not understand why they had such a bond the drinking could not have been the only reason. Then again, she had to be his enabler too. She was on the scene years ago when we were in the house in North Philly. "*Momma said*", *"never feel sorry for a man, you may have baby momma drama".*

Anyway, I would hear from his sister that he would go and confront her and tell her to stop calling but she was too hurt that he would marry me and not her. Strangely, I began to feel some type of compassion for her. I knew in my heart that he was leading her on, using her and lying to her.

I actually spoke to him and told him that he should not do that to her it was not right. I believe I told him to let her go on with her life, he had made his decision to marry me. I actually heard that he beat her up for calling the house and my job. Was I suppose to be glad? No. I was not that immature and cold-hearted. I felt sorry for her and sorry for myself. *Momma said," "never feel sorry for a man, you may actually have compassion for the other woman. "Strange I know.*

At some point the calls stopped and we went on to pretend that we were happy. I worked at my job at Amtrak up until late December 1993. The next day, on my way to work, my water broke as I was walking to the bus stop. I turned around and went back into the house. I called my husband and refused to go to the hospital until he got there. What was that about? Maybe because he was not there when our daughter was born, I allowed my pride to get in the way. I was not working my recovery, I had relapsed.

I knew it was dangerous to not go straight to the hospital if there was any sign of the water bag breaking. But I still waited and called the Dr instead of going to the hospital. Some hours had passed and he was not home yet from work. The Dr. actually called me to see if I was coming in. Now that is insanity, when the Dr. has to tell you to come in. After waiting all day, I decided to call a cab and take the trip alone. The pains were still maybe 3 to 5 minutes apart. I thought I was a pro after having three babies already. I was a little arrogant too as you could see.

I don't remember much about arriving at the hospital besides being placed in a room waiting to have the baby. My husband came in the room with the children. I was so disappointed in him. He was not a good support coach, he actually looked at me while I was in labor and said, "give her hell son." ***"Momma said, "Never feel sorry for a man he may not be there for you when you need him the most." "He may not know how to be compassionate."***

I was discharged the next day, with our beautiful baby boy, I waited for D.C. to arrive with a friend who had bought him in his car. Well he had come through this time, and had the baby seat too. It was a snowy stormy day. I was very concerned about the weather, hoping that we would make it home safe. Thank God we made it home and there was my little girls welcoming their new baby brother. It was nice to finally have a son, after having three girls.

I was a proud mother again, and doing what a mother is suppose to do, take care of her children. I have always struggled taking care of me; although I was good at taking care of others. I was concerned about my youngest daughter who had gotten use to being the youngest. Unfortunately, daddy wanted me to have a son. He did not treat her like daddy's precious little girl as I feel men should do.

Maybe some women would do better at choosing a partner and setting boundaries in their relationships and standards, If they had a good daddy or male role model by their side. Just a thought .... ***Momma said, "never feel sorry for a man, he may not be grateful for the blessing of being able to conceive a children."***

The reality is he had babies by other women and most of them had girls, so he was not impressed by God's choice. I did have two step-sons, but had only met one. He had no real respect for women. He did not have a happy relationship with his own mother, most of the time he was subconsciously, angry with her. Although I know he loved her, he just wished she was home more to nurture him.

She used school to escape from her emotional pain, well that is the impression that he gave me. He spent a lot of time being raised by his sister and the streets. He turned into a rolling stone, where ever he laid his hat/or left some clothes was his home. **Momma said, "never feel sorry for a man, he may not know the value of a woman."**

My husband was not home most of the time, and when he did come home he went upstairs and off to bed. My job gave me six months to return, I did not want to put the baby in daycare that soon. I resigned and decided to start my own business as a Daycare Provider in my home. After taking some classes and getting some paper work in order, It was done. It was three long years but a great experience. I was determined that I would be a professional daycare provider, not just a baby sister.

I did not sit home watching soaps; I planned the day from beginning to the end. The children had their meals and lessons and fun, and then would go home. By the way, since I did not go to Kindergarten, I had some fun with those children and Barney too. My after-school children would come in and I would feed them a snack and help with homework too. It was exhausting. But I loved it.

I learned something about myself during this experience; I was a business women. The experiences that we go through in life are suppose to help build character and most of all show us our strengths and weaknesses. I was learning to accept myself. As the children grew and began to go to school this included my son and three daughters, I decided to volunteer at the school.

I kept volunteering and trying to get my neighbor to do the same. She had found the courage some years ago to get out of her abusive relationship. She had been stomped by her children's father and even had some teeth missing. She was so smart and isolated with her three children. Most times she did not leave the house, not unless it was time to pay bills and shop for food. She never did volunteer at the school. ***Momma said" never feel sorry for a man, you could lose your self-esteem and not see yourself as valuable.***

Her children and my children became best of friends, we lived across the hall from each-other. We were both blessed with bi-level apartments. We had the third and fourth floors. One and a half bath and 3 bedrooms. I knew God had given me favor when I qualified for this place.

When I first got the place my husband was not suppose to move in with me. I did not want the drama in my life that he was bringing. But instead I decided to let him move in after he made some promises to get some help and decided to go with me one night to bible study. Rev. Rice said, "he would be saved tonight.

My husband got on his knees at the alter and repented and gave his life to Christ. That only lasted for a short time. He respected Rev. Rice and would get in touch with him now and then. Rev Rice, passed away. My husband's old behaviors surfaced again and his heart was not changed. ***Momma said, "never feel sorry for a man he will go to church with you but will not truly allow his heart and mind to be changed. Momma also said, "a man will say anything a woman wants to hear to get what he wants.***

*I had decided to start working my recovery again at home, but was not attending meetings.* I was also getting up early and watching the Christian TV station. My mind was being renewed. I was learning how to accept the love of God. I was learning how to love and accept myself, shortcomings and all the bad choices I had made. I was learning that I had so many strengths, gifts, intelligence and I was lovable and loving.

I had been a caretaker for many years, but did not know how to take care of myself, emotionally, spiritually or physically. *I can be a caretaker, as long as it's done in a healthy way and I don't forget about myself.* My children as well as others some time need my support. *Do not do for others what they can do for themselves. Anything can get out of balance.* **Momma said, "never feel sorry for a man, you may feel like you are raising another child."**

I was also learning how to love and accept others. I had learned that I could not change others, but I could set healthy boundaries for myself. I could let God work in me and change me. I learned how to be humble and accept the fact that I needed God in my life in all areas. I was not perfect. **Momma said, "never feel sorry for a man, you may put him over your relationship with the God that created you and sent His Son to die for YOU."**

I decided to take some college classes. Maybe I could become a Drug and Alcohol Counselor. I could not help the man I had married, maybe I could help someone that wanted the help. I would put the kids in bed and then exercise. I needed to shed those extra pounds. *I had been an emotional eater for a long time.* Then I would study. I went to class across the street from my home and one class I had to take at the campus on Spring Garden Street. *It felt good; I had taken some control over my life.*

My husband was not very happy about me taking classes, and attending support group meetings again. I met knew people and went to special anniversaries for those who were doing well in recovery. I remember stepping into my first meeting in West Philly in 1993. I felt so alone.

I had been stuffing my feelings for so long, that most of the time I felt anxiety instead of peace. *As I continued to allow myself to feel my feelings instead of running from them I found peace. I did this also by accepting when I was angry or sad or whatever feelings I was having.* When I got busy I got better according to the Ala non literature. So I began to do service. A friend introduced me to doing service at the prison in Philly as well. We actually took a meeting to the women inmates. It went well, although I did not like the spirit of the prison. I prayed before I went in.

Each area had it's own group name. My group had been around for over 40 years. It was great being apart of a group with so much history. Some of the members knew the two gentlemen God used to start this awesome support group back in the 50's. All the other groups started as a result of these two men that were willing to trust God and change. I made new friends, and felt more in control. I laughed more and learned how to make time for me, besides taking care of my family.

My husband was still not a happy camper. He did not seem to like my new life. He liked the needy me, the insecure me, the angry me, the fearful me. He would continue to drink and stay out a night or sometimes two. I stopped arguing with him. I knew there would come a day when I would find the strength and faith to let him go.

One night, while the children were in bed, and I was at the table studying, he came home. He was very quite I think he had a beer in his hand. He sat at the table. I spoke to him, but had an uneasy feeling in my stomach. He looked at the books on the table, he began to ask questions about the pictures and what the book said.

He seemed to know that It was about alcoholism and addictive behaviors.

I answered his question; he sat quietly in the chair in deep thought sometimes watching me. Then I saw a tear stream down from the side of his eye. Some say that is a sign of anger. Anyway, I asked him what was wrong and if he wanted to talk about it. He did not say anything, I told him I was going to check the children.

As I began to go up the stairs he yelled to me, "don't go up those stairs"! I could feel the fear in my stomach. I did not know whether to run up the stairs on come back. I knew if I ran he would catch me so I decided to come back and try to calm him down.

I could not calm him down, once again he sat quietly in the chair looking at me. I stood in front of him trying to figure out what to say next. He leaped out of the chair like a cobra with a grip on my neck. He was backing me up into the kitchen cabinet and choking me. I was off guard and beginning to black out. It's called a black out but I saw something like clouds.

I heard my children running down the stairs, and then my son standing next to him, he loosed his grip. As our son stared at him choking me, I signaled to him to look down, he shouted "I don't give a f—k. Then my oldest daughter ran up to him and hit him with the broom. This startled him, he pushed away and went after her, and pushed her down. The other girls were yelling, I reached for the phone to call the police, he knocked it out of my hand. I got to the neighbor's home across the hall. I called the police and he ran out the building.

When I knew he was gone we went back to our place. It was a snowy night, I looked from the third floor window of my apartment. I could see him at the phone booth on top of the El train platform. I called my brother to come and get the kids and I.

My husband called me and I kept him on the phone and signaled for the children to get there coats and things together. He told me that he had nothing to lose after I had chosen to call the police on him, knowing that he was already on parole. I must admit that statement took me back to the trauma of my childhood and what we experienced in our home. I called my brother, he and his wife were on their way.

The police came, I filed a statement and left for my brother's home. I felt so numb and disappointed for being at my brothers house. I was good at keeping family out of my business. I was embarrassed and was use to handling things on my own. In the past, my husband use to dare me to call my brothers and I would never do it. I did not want any one to get hurt. I would have blamed myself. I knew he was crazy. **Momma said, "never feel sorry for a man, he may try to kill you, maybe in front of your children."**

I did not want to stay at my brother's home and at the same time was afraid to go home. I did what I was use to doing, I spoke to him on the phone and he calmed down and apologized. He promised to get some help. After a day or two we went back home. I know my brother and his wife was concerned for us. I guess I was behaving like my mother; when we were growing up. She use to say, she was not leaving her home for nobody. It was not the home; I did not want us to be a burden on them. I would figure something out.

Crazy as it may seem we went on as if it never happened. I had heard stories of alcoholics having blackouts. I had learned of this while reading the Ala-non literature but never thought it would happen to us. My husband use to tell me stories that his father told him that he saw him walking down his street in his underwear but I had never seen it. I did not want to believe it either.

One morning, we were having breakfast and my husband was up in the bedroom. My oldest daughter went upstairs to see if he wanted breakfast. She came downstairs acting a bit strange but did not express any emotions. Some time passed and she was in the hall way with a friend talking. They both came to me and told me a shocking story.

She told me that when she entered the room he shut the door and she had to kick him to stop him from attacking her in the worst way. I asked her if he had rapped her and she said know. But she was upset and crying. She said she had never seen him like that. She said his voice changed and his eyes changed colors. Then he leaped after her. Fortunately, she was able to get away and confide in a friend.

She was afraid to tell me not knowing how I would act. I went upstairs to confront him. He cried saying that he did not remember any of it. He apologized to her and promised to get some help and he left.

I grew up knowing that you don't let a man do anything to your kids.

My mother would not have it, we never got a beating from any of our step dads, and they had better not have looked at us girls in the wrong way, my mother would lose it.

Strangely I never new much about her past, but later found out that while she was young she was rapped by two brothers that was suppose to be friends that she trusted. I never met my grandmother on my mother's side. She had a nervous breakdown and was taken out of the home. My mother was still a child at the time.

My mother's father was an alcoholic as well. He did not make it in the rooms of AA (Alcoholics Anonymous). If only my grandmother had gotten a chance to get into a recovery program or had knowledge that there was hope and help available for her. **Momma** *said, "never feel sorry for a man you could end up having a nervous breakdown."*

My husband signed himself into a program. He was on blackout for a few weeks, meaning he could not talk to family and friends not even on the phone. He stayed in a halfway house for a few months.

He seemed to be doing better sober for some time. An old court case finally surfaced. This was from a few years ago when he was a lookout for the drug dealers in North Philly. He did not have a job at the time and I told him that he had to get one and he got one. That would have not been my choice.

Strangely he had his priorities, he would not touch the drugs nor bring it in the house. But one day he got busted passing drugs from one person to another. That was not even in his job description. *Momma said, "never feel sorry for a man, you might end up in court with him."*

He was found guilty and placed on house arrest for maybe 3 months. He actually had a real job during this time as a roofer. He was allowed to go to work and back. He had this little black box around his ankle. It was connected to a computer system. Who ever monitored the system knew how far he had gone. They could pick him up if he was out of range or, especially if he took it off. He could shower but not take a bath.

It was the only time I actually felt secure and could trust him. I knew where he was, who he was with and when he was coming home. He behaved some what normal such as: sitting downstairs and watching TV with us and some times having dinner downstairs and not in the bedroom. *Momma said, "never feel sorry for a man, you may only feel secure with him in the relationship when he is on house arrest."*

59

He seemed a little uncomfortable with this new lifestyle he was only use to being home a few days at a time. He was a different person when he was running the street life. He would be the loudest one in the bar. I thought he could not dance and one night a few years before, we went out and he was a good latino dancer. I did not know whether to be happy or angry that he seemed to be living a double life. I always loved to dance. That night was the first time we had ever danced seriously. ***Momma said" never feel sorry for a man, you may not know who he really is."***

I thought he would lose his mind in the house for 3 months but he seemed to handle it well. He probably needed the break. The addiction of alcohol controls the person more than the person controlling the addiction and the behaviors that comes along with it. I guess he was grateful that he was not sent to prison.

I believe he had to take a drug test every so often so drinking was almost out of the picture until he found something that would flush out the occasional beer. After the 3 months was over he slowly went back into his old life style. I reminded him of his recovery and he arrogantly told me that he had already gotten help. ***Momma said, "never feel sorry for a man", he may not realize that recovery is a life long journey."***

He began to stay out all night again not the usual two nights just one. He would come home with change of clothes and his old clothes folded and smelling Downy fresh. I would ask him who washed his clothes and he would not tell me. He would look at me wanting to know what I had cooked for dinner.

I would get angry and tell him he had a lot of nerve to ask me that. He retreat to the bedroom. I would not go up if I thought we would argue. I was learning in recovery to choose my battles and take care of myself.

I waited for the right time to approach him. I also waited until he was not drunk, which may have been the next day. God and recovery had given me the courage to realize I had choices. He had broken all of the vows. I did not have to deal with his behavior.

I went up to the bedroom, I sat on the bed and told him we needed to talk. I directly, not angrily, told him that he had the right to live his life which ever way he chose. I told him in so many words that I did not want a marriage that I did not feel secure in and a man that I could not trust and did not honor me.

I asked him to leave, he was not happy about it but said ok. He did not leave right way, he once told me that he was not leaving, and I had assured him that he would. He went to sleep and I did not bother him. We talked again, and he asked me if he could stay until Saturday. This was earlier in the week, maybe a Monday. So I said yes, because I knew he would have money then. See old habits are hard to break. *Was I still enabling him?*

*Two days later, he* was back at his roofing job. I was home caring for my son and another child as I continued to take my classes part time. On Thursday October 22nd 1997 he got up for work. I would usually make his lunch and watch from the third floor window as he went to the car or the train station. I use to get up with him to see him off to work. Trying to be the perfect wife to a man that was not a good husband to me. Besides I wanted to watch Christian TV.

Sometimes he just chose not to take the car, it was old. On the days he would take the train I would wonder if the young lady from downstairs was on the train with him. They had seemed to get pretty close over the past weeks.

Her mother and I were friends. She had bonded with my husband also and she thought he was checking on her. He had other motives

It seemed. You know we usually know when our men have their eye on another woman, Or who they are attracted to.

He was the one who told me that she would be on the train going the same way and that they would talk. He acted as if it was no big deal. It didn't bother me until her mother told me that he was knocking on her door. I knew he was not doing that before. So of course I was concerned. **Momma said, "never feel sorry for a man, he may honor another woman over you." It might be your friend. DON'T let her move in.**

Now back to October 22nd, two days before he was suppose to move out. This day he took the car and I watched as he drove off. I was so hurt from him staying out a few days before that. I almost did not pray for him. I usually prayed for him as he left for work. I knew not praying for him was not good and I felt the Holy Spirit telling me to pray for him so I did. God said, "love is not selfish". It's not all about me, even when I am hurting.

Later, that afternoon, I received a phone call from the hospital. It was a nurse, she told me that my husband had hit his head and was asking for me. I did not drive at this time; I told me neighbor to watch the child I was taking care of after calling the mother. My son who was four at this time, and I walked over to Spruce Street and took the bus.

I arrived at University Hospital and went to the Emergency Ward. I told someone at the front desk who I was and asked if I could see my husband. I was given a strange look and told to go to the Chaplain's office. She would be with me soon. I said, "the Chaplain"! "Is my husband dead of alive"! "I was told that he had a bump on his head and was asking for me." The person on the phone had lied to me. I would not have bought my son if I thought it was a life or death situation.

I went into the Chaplain's office and waited. A women walked in with long dreadlocks. She introduced herself as Ramona the Chaplain. That's my name! I began to feel the presence of God. She had a very nice personality. I asked her how was my husband? She told me that first they needed to determine if he was my husband. Oh, I was hoping that it wasn't. **Momma said, "never feel sorry for a man, your whole world may turn upside down in a day."**

She described a man with short dread locks and an Aries tattoo on his arm. I began to cry, she told me that he was in surgery and that his head injury was fatal. He had lost most of the blood in his body and needed a blood transfusion. His head was split open and his brain exposed.

I was told that he had just come back from lunch. He was working on the roof of a smaller hospital in another area under a crane and it fell on his head. He had to be taken to another hospital by helicopter.

I forgot about all the anger and hurt from my marriage. I looked at her and grabbed her by the hands and told her that he was not going out like this. I began to pray for him to make it through the surgery and he made it. I called my family, and my sister in-law came to pick up my son.

My mother came to the hospital and some family members for support. Some of his co-workers were explaining what they saw. I could tell they were traumatized, but wanted to support me as best they knew how. One of his friends was giving me some advice. I was watching everybody and numb at the same time. Could this really be happening?

His mother and father arrived. Everyone was shocked and just wanted to know if he would live. I tried hard not to imagine myself as a widow. It would have been easy to think the worse since I suffered trauma from my own childhood.

But it was not about me now, my husband's life was on the edge.

Hours later, we were told that he made it through the surgery. What a relief, but we knew it was very serious. We could not see him right away.

My girls were home in shock; actually they were at my neighbor's home across the hall. I felt bad that I could not be there for them during their moments of fear and anxiety. Wow, you never know which way life will turn.

I still had my four year old son with me. We were finally able to see him. It was shocking. His face was swollen and his head was very big and bandaged of course. I felt no anger towards him only compassion.

I am sure *I was not feeling my feelings,* this was usually one of my coping behaviors since childhood. But I knew at this time it was not about me. My son, so adorable, who seemed like a little adult, held his father's hand and said, "daddy you will be alright".

My heart went out to both of them. Other family members were allowed to go in and out for a short time, but only two at a time. We were not allowed to say in the ICU for long. We were told to go home. I have very little memory of when happened when I went home.

I do know that my girls needed an explanation, they thought that the only dad they really knew was dead. Well I had two by him, but the other two was his step-children, by marriage. One was only six months old when we met and the other was around 4.

He treated them as his own, he loved them too although sadly he seemed to some times criticize the daughter I had by him making her feel rejected. I believe it was his opinion about the women in his family. His issues of course. She is so beautiful and looks just like him. I call her my chocolate baby.

Him being in this accident changed our whole life. The next day I went to visit him and there were balloons and cards left for him. I read the card it was from a woman named Denise. I knew about Sandra but not Denise. Of course, I could not confront him.

He spent a few months in the hospital in Philadelphia and then he went into a rehab facility. I did my research and chose the best one for victims of brain trauma. He was paralyzed on his left side and had some brain damage mostly short term memory loss. *Momma said, "never feel sorry for a man, the unknown may happen." Let Go and let God.*

I would visit him daily and bring my son with me. His progress was a miracle. I was not too surprised considering I had called everyone I knew to pray for him including: some prayer hotlines and TV ministries. I would never know all the people that prayed for him. Well maybe when I get to Heaven.

During the day my son and I were allowed to go to most of his therapies with him and my son would push him in the wheel chair. Being four years old he enjoyed the experience. After school some days I would go and get the girls and bring them to visit.

I would come back the next day and there would be something from Denise left behind a business card or something. The phone would ring and I would answer and it was usually a hangup or just breathing on the phone. Sometimes, I would come in and he would be on the phone.

I restricted his visitors to myself, his mother and close family members only. That did not work because his mother was under minding me behind my back. **Momma said "never feel sorry for a man, you may not have a mother in law that is trustworthy."**

It became difficult emotionally. I would confront him about his women visits and we would go in the bathroom and I would express my anger. Although, I had told him the same week of his accident, he had to move out; he was still my husband and I wanted to be respected and appreciated for being there for him in spite of everything. **Momma said, "life is not fair."**

I was hoping that this terrible accident somehow would be a wakeup call for him, but unfortunately, it wasn't. During one of our arguments he looked me right in my face and told me that he would be doing the same thing he was doing if it had not been for the accident. **Momma said, "never feel sorry for a man not even a tragedy can make him change."**

Insanity had come back. I started hiding the phone receiver in the drawer knowing that he could not reach it after I left. He would ask someone to get it for him. What was I thinking? I needed a healthy support system.

I needed to find a way to take back my power the best way I knew how. I believed someday he was going to come home and I would choose to take care of him. It was hard to leave him in this condition. But I felt so stuck. Lord, what do I do?

I had planned to get my tubes tied just in case he could make another baby. I decided to go through with it. I needed to feel like I had some control. For one day I did not visit him because of my short procedure.

The day of my procedure I received a call from the Social Worker informing me that a women had showed up although his visitors had been restricted to family only. She told me that she had asked the woman if she knew he was married, she said yes that she was meeting his mother. I was so disappointed with my mother-in law. I had trusted her. **Momma said, "never feel sorry for a man his mother may think that enabling is loyalty."**

I felt my recovery had either gone out the window or I had relapsed. I was suppose to be learning how to take care of myself. What a mess. I going to less meetings. My recovery friends knew all about the accident and were very understanding. But I needed to be running to more meetings instead of going to less.

There were times when I would have meetings with his Social Worker and Neurologist. It was a requirement of the program and rehab he was in. Theresa and Lynette were always very nice to me and showed compassion. I appreciated their support. They had gotten use to my children and I coming to the rehab. They told me that many women had left their husband's at the rehab and have never looked back. They seem to commend me for hanging in there. They looked concerned for me. I could not see myself doing that. I felt I was doing what was right. **Momma said, "never feel sorry for a man you could love him more than you love your self."**

*After four* months my husband was doing so well that he was transferred to an upgraded rehabilitation facility for those with brain injuries. They would teach him how to become more independent. They were going to teach him also how to live on his own if he had to.

The word had gotten out about our dysfunctional marriage. This facility had certain rules that I had to abide by such as: we could no longer visit daily. We could only visit once a week. They did not want him to be dependent on me anymore. ***Hmmmm was this God working on my behalf?***

I had not accepted the fact that maybe it was ok for me to move on. I started looking for a house that would be handicap accessible. I was just going through the motions and carrying so much pain and anger and resentment. I was obsessing in my mind and being reminded of what he had told me some time ago. He said to me that he would be doing the same things if it had not been for the accident. ***Truth sets us free.***

That was my wakeup call; he did not want to change. I was depressed. I went to a support group meeting, but nothing seemed to help. I was in Center City Philly and decided to take a walk over to Rittenhouse Square. I found a park bench. I sat and watched as people seemed to stop and smell the roses, something that I had not done in months. ***Momma said, "never feel sorry for a man you may not slow down to feel your feelings." Feeling is healing.***

While I was sitting on the bench a tall woman walked over to me and asked if she could sit down. I said no to myself; I did not want to be bothered. But did chose not to say no to her. I was use to isolating when I felt numb or depressed or anxious. I was hoping that she did not start talking to me but she did.

She began to talk about her son and the crisis that was going on in her relationship with him. I began to listen, thinking maybe I could be of help just by listening to her. Of course, this set me up to talk as well. She seemed sincere, although I thought she was a little crazy at first.

I found myself telling this stranger about my husband's accident and the troubles in our marriage. She looked at me strangely and said, "honey God has already moved this man from your life; do you need him"? I thought to myself how could I possibly need a man that had no respect for me nor himself. ***Momma said, "never feel sorry for a man he may not honor his vows".***

I looked at her and said no, but I felt guilty for leaving him. God had worked things out for him. He was in a good place. I had seen him do things in recovery that I had never seen him do in all the years we were together. While still in his wheelchair he would roll to the kitchen and make a sandwich. He would leave me in his room and go to the laundry room to check his clothes.

I was amazed and happy for him. This program had done a great job in rehabilitating him. I thought he would still be in the wheel chair; I could not find a home that was wheelchair accessible. But eventually, he did not need the wheelchair, just a cane. Wow! I guess it was God, because after my conversation with the stranger in the park I knew I had to let go or die. ***Momma said, "never feel sorry for a man you may lose your life."***

After that women spoke to me, I felt a weight lift off of my shoulders after speaking to her. I really felt something leave me. I truly believe God had sent me an angel. I followed her to the bus stop after I got my break through right there in the park. I did not want her to leave. I was no longer depressed. I knew it was God's divine intervention. ***I needed to trust God with his life. I was not his God nor his mother. I needed to trust God with my life.***

He had to leave this facility program. I told him I was filing for divorce and he decided to get himself a townhouse. I had never been there although his mother would visit him and so would some staff from the program. He was doing well on his own most of the time. His friends would visit, even my oldest daughter and step son had gone to see him.

It had been four years so many things had changed. I decided to move the children from the city to NJ. It was a blessing from something that appeared to be a curse. God had chosen to be good to us all. I was a single mother again it felt strange. He was not coming home this time.

We were going through the divorce and it was difficult. I could not believe that we were not together anymore. I had forgiven him but still had a lot of healing to do. Sometimes in our hearts we have not let go. We had been together for ten years.

A few years later, one night the children and I were in bed. I was in my room almost asleep when my children ran into my room shouting, "daddy's dead" daddy's dead"! I felt instantly numb. Fear had hit me. I could not believe it. I wondered what happened after he had survived such an horrific accident five years ago.

Sadly to say he had been dead a few days before we found out. His mother and some other family members did not want us to know, for selfish reasons. My oldest daughter had received a phone call from my step-sons mother. She had run into a friend who had told her. I knew it was God's divine intervention again.

I was hurt and upset and so were the children. I asked his mother what had happened and she claimed it to be stress. In reality she was trying to make me feel guilty for filing for divorce. I realized that as his wife I still had rights. I made some calls including the funeral home and told them who I was.

I asked them what happened and I was told that he had died from blood clots to his heart and lungs. I believe that it was because he was smoking and taking those blood thinners which had been a previous concern for me. He and his mother had returned from church. He was eating and began to choke and his life ended.

I was told by his mother that I was not allowed to come to the funeral. I told her that I would be there. I was furious with her. I did not understand her behavior. How as a women could she not understand what I had gone through with her son? I called my lawyer and he suggested that I not go. We had been separated for some time. **Momma said, "never feel sorry for a man, when you finally let go even his family won't understand.'**

I made arrangements for my sister-in law to take the children for me. I stayed with my two nieces. I decided to take them to get their nails done.

It was a sad day, I actually worried about him even after death. I prayed and asked God if he had made it to Heaven. When the children returned I was told that he was buried with a cigarette in his mouth.

I was also told that his sister wrote a poem for him. I read the eulogy and It gave me comfort that just maybe he made it to Heaven. I heard that he had started attending church and he bought the bibles for his mother's church. Hopefully, he gave his heart to Christ too. **Momma said, "never feel sorry for a man, you may worry about him even after he is gone."**

# Chapter 8

## The NightClub Escape

I carried so much disappointment from the marriage. I could not believe it was over and he was gone. How could he die after all of that rehab and treatments? I knew it was God's mercy that he lived five years after his accident. But I was blaming God for allowing things to end like this. I had put so much time and energy into the relationship. **Momma said, never feel sorry for a man it may be hard to let go when it's over."**

At some point I had started going out with my sister. It started on a Sunday night with the oldies dance party. Then Thursday night at the club in West Philly and then Monday nights at a different location. I was depressed again. How could I put this all behind me? I was a widow? I had never imagined being a widow.

My partying had spiraled out of control. I began to date other men. Of course my choices in men had not changed. I had a lot of fun with the young and older ones. I dated a police detective after my sister insisted that he kept asking about me. He had major issues from his past marriage. It appeared that he was allowing his ex-wife use the kids to control him, although she had moved on with someone else.

He was afraid of commitment appearing to be satisfied with the honey-moon stage of the relationship. In other words he was just a player. It ended after a few months. He stopped calling and when I got back to the club he was sitting with another woman. He looked at me so kindly and called my name to say hello. I could not believe he thought I would be comfortable with this. I wanted to slap him, but refused to allow myself to look like a fool. Learning the lesson was better although feeling the disappointment was tough. ***Momma said, "never feel sorry for a man, he may use you, then say "next".***

Then I met another young man. He was a divorcee who had moved back in with his mother. He too seemed to have emotional issues from his past relationship. His ex-wife was older than he and was also an alcoholic. Well that was something that we both had in common. Maybe we both had Coda issues as well. You think?

I liked the way we met. It was Monday night at Kelly Drive. My sister and I had decided to as a girlfriend of mine to come with us because it was her birthday. I was focused on her having a good time. I saw this guy. He was dressed nicely but casual and cute. I asked him if he would dance with my friend. He said yes. I felt proud of myself, I was a match maker.

It turned out that she was not interested in him, but he was interested in me. Now believe it or not I was shocked. That was not part of the plan. I began to talk to him and excused myself for a line dance or two. He seemed to enjoy watching me dance. I was always a good dancer.

We began to date and it was nice and romantic in the beginning. That was something that I had not known for some time. It felt

73

good, but these good feelings led me into another unhealthy relationship. Although he tried to hide it he too was abusive and controlling. He was also very insecure. Funny how we take the small things that are not as important and dismiss our standards. ***Momma said" never feel sorry for a man you may become disillusioned by your emotions."***

Unfortunately, he also had abandonment issues. He would sometime disappear, actually I felt he was rejecting me. It would happen at strange times for example we would be on the phone, I thought the conversation was going good, but when I did not agree with him he would shift. I was direct and I am a bottom line person. He would stop calling and answering my calls.

I believe it must have turned him off or he got the message that he could not control me. So he began to back away from the relationship, but in a very immature way. I actually thought we were still a couple and maybe he was upset about something although I did not know what it was.

He would leave me hanging. I would wait a few days and then a week. He would surface briefly and we would talk. Then I would find out that I said something that he did not like or made him feel insecure or rejected. It was like being in a relationship with a teenager. M***omma said, "never feel sorry for a man, he may reject you before you get a chance to reject him.***

This Houdini act was getting tiresome. I would call his mother's home where he was staying. Yea, I know, now. He would tell his mother to tell me that he was going to call me back, but never did. I felt as if I was on an emotional roller coaster. I believe he had studied women and realized that we need communication, so this was his way of punishing me by playing with my emotions. At least I saw it this way. I guess I refused to believe that he was that immature. Closure would have felt better, show some respect.

74

**"What made me think that I did not have the power to just end the relationship?"**

I called a few months later, and His mother told me that he was on his honeymoon. I was devastated. I took it really hard. I was so angry with him. I did not understand his behavior. Was I not worth the respect to just end the relationship? **Momma said, "never feel sorry for a man, he may marry someone else and not give you closure."**

I called him the next day when he got back to work. I asked him when was he going to let me know that he had gotten married? He arrogantly, said to me, "I was going to tell you". I was so angry with him, I wanted to go to his job and slap him. Almost did, but not a good idea. **Momma said, "never feel sorry for a man he may selfishly disregard your feelings."**

Finally, I was able to let go and start my healing process once again. I had this habit of jumping from one relationship to another. I met an adorable guy named JM. I was at the club on oldies night, this time in NJ. I was at the bar talking and there was this cute guy with dreads watching me. I walked by and he blocked my path. That is when I realized that he wanted to meet me. He was slim and handsome and younger.

We began to talk and eventually became friends. We got along too well. He was a musician. I thought that was different. His parents were in Ministry and they decided to move to Florida. He had a sister, although I don't remember meeting her. The relationship was nice but going no where. I later realized that he cared for me more then I knew.

He was not the guy that was looking for a wife. Although much later he mentioned to a friend that he would have chosen me. You know that fed my ego, but the reality was he was not the settling down type. He was planning to travel to England. ***Momma said, "never feel sorry for a man, he may not be looking for a wife."***

Eventually I was the one that moved away, and he was not happy about it.

I began to feel a lot of conviction about the life I was living. I was a back-slidden Christian and needed to repent and get right with God. After all of my drinking and dancing and dating. I took a look at my life and felt God calling me back to Him. I answered the call. I am glad I did, if not I would not be writing this book today.

I am grateful for God's grace and mercy and patience. He knew that I was not happy in the club. He would actually allow me to step back from time to time and just watch the people in the crowd. I saw hurting, lonely, people, seeking attention and putting on a front. I saw big egos and I had one. I would walk in the club as If I was a queen. I knew my admirers were there. I was playing the role myself. I was one of them.

For a while it felt good but it was time to run back into my daddy's arms.

I had never completely turned away from God. I prayed daily but with a lot of guilt, shame, and condemnation. I knew I was oppressed. I spoke to God about my inner most feelings. I cried out to God for help.

I would go for a drive and park my car and speak to God. I felt as if I had tried everything. I had always wanted to make a difference in the world. I was blessed to be a Crisis Hotline Counselor as well as take recovery bibles to the prison in Philadelphia, and help as many youth and people as God would allow me to. That person began to surface again.

I had surrendered to God. I had the beautiful home; it had been almost four years since we had moved to NJ. We had family get togethers and great memories. I felt there was more to life as I always have. I needed more and began to pray about my purpose. I told God I would go where ever He sent me, just like He told Moses and so many others in the bible. Within a short period of time strange things began to happen.

# Chapter 9

## *A New Journey in St Lucia*

I had learned not to get too attached to anything or anyone that did not die on the cross for me. That also included family and friends. *In other words we are not to love anything or anyone more than God.* I had begun a new journey. Although God was shifting me I did not feel it right away. It's as if I had forgotten about my prayer and promise to God, but He did not forget.

It was almost Spring 2004. I remember my daughter Inez wanted to get her hair done in kinky twist; they were popular at the time. We had no idea who could do the job. We were shopping at Best Buy and somehow this guy stopped me to give me a flyer for a show, I believe a hair show. I do remember that we somehow got on a conversation about Inez's hair. He said he had a friend that could do it for her. No coincidences with God.

He gave me her number and we called her. Let's say her name was Ms. Aries. She sounded like a serious person over the phone. We made an appointment to meet with her. We drove over I believe the next day. She was loving but had a strong personality. We had to wait until she opened the Salon. Somehow we got on a spiritual conversation.

She said she was a member of a church and there was some people that had really hurt her. I could still see the hurt in her eyes. She said she had a gift of prophesy but some of the church members was giving her a hard time about it and she left that particular church. She was a single mother in her late twenties.

I left Inez with her to get her hair done. I came back several hours later to check on them. To my surprise, my daughter said all Ms. Aries did was talk about me. Inez seemed amazed at some of the things she was saying. I wanted to know what she had to say although I was a little skeptical. She did not know me.

I waited in the SUV for my daughter to come out. Ms. Aries came over to the window. She was smiling and seemed very sure about what she was saying. She told me that I was going to have a house by the water. She told me that I was moving. I did not know what she was talking about.

She told me that I was going to meet a man and be by his side. That scared me a little because I did not know did that mean he was going to be by my side.

Of course, fear showed up. I left my daughter with her and went for a drive. I began to pray and speak to God. I told God that I was afraid and I did not understand but never the less I wanted His will to be done. I picked up my daughter and decided to let it go.

A few months later I was home on my computer. I had wanted to take another trip. I had already taken my mother and daughter to Hawaii. I had also taken my mother on a cruise to Cancun Mexico. During that time she was in a lot of pain and waiting to have back surgery but decided to go on the trip.

I did not know she was in so much pain. I would have chosen a trip with less walking. It was my first cruise as well. The cruise ships are very large territory to cover. She was a real trooper determined not to let the pain get the best of her. We managed to have a nice time then some months later.

I was on the computer then I heard this island music and saw two of my favorite artists at the time, called Floetry. They were two neo-soul singing sisters from England and they were going to be in some island called St. Lucia. I called Air Jamaica, booked a flight for two. Then I called my sister to see if she wanted to go. My mind was made up; I wanted to see Floetry.

She had never heard of St Lucia, neither did I. I remember before I had planned the trip I had gotten a desire to travel to the West indies. It was so strong that I started telling people. I knew It was in the Caribbean and that was good enough for me. I loved islands and wanted to travel again.

When I was a teen girl, I loved Geography I was curious about this little body of land surrounded by water. It amazed me that people could live there. I use to trace the maps and just stare at the picture poster on the wall in the classroom. Never dreaming that someday I would visit such a beautiful place; much less live there. God does place good desires in us and guides our steps. Maybe that is one reason why we are to learn from our past instead of regretting it. *God knows everything we are going to do before we do it. We are not a surprise to Him.*

A few months went by and in May we were on our way to St Lucia. Funny we got to the airport and because there was only one flight they decided to leave early. We were disappointed but decided to stay in the hotel near the airport and book another flight for the following day.

All went well the next day and off to St Lucia we went. It was a very nice resort in Castries, which was near town. The island music was nothing like I was use to but very nice. My sister and I had noticed the beauty of the decor that also included trying one of those island drinks. I know . . . I know. I was slowly *coming* out of my backslidden state.

I felt kind of sad and decided to just sit in a chair and relax. I was not dressed as If I was on vacation. I was still depressed but keeping my head up. I had on a jean skirt and a casual top. But for some reason that night I did not care to much about how I looked. I just wanted to get away. My sister met a young man named Tom. Later, I met a young man named Wayne. They both worked at the resort.

Tom and my sister got along very nicely and so did Wayne and I. He was in his late twenties. I know what was I doing? Wayne was working and I was relaxing. When he got a moment we began to talk. Somehow we got on a spiritual conversation.

The atmosphere began to shift. He said to me that so many people come to visit the island and only see the resorts but there was a lot of hurting people out side of the resorts. When he said that God spoke to me. I felt compassion come over me. I believe God was telling me I could make a difference here.

I was tired and went to bed. The next day I was looking forward to seeing Floetry but we had a lot of rain and the concert actually got rained out. Rumor said, that they were at some club. I had given up the club life, so I refused to go. Strangely I was there a whole week and never got a chance to see Floetry. God laughs at our plans.

I met a young man named Brian he was a cook. I really liked him we got a long good and he would come out of the kitchen to give me extra attention. I loved it. As time went on I realized he had several children. He also had more than one baby momma. Oh no! **Momma said, "never feel sorry for a man you may end up with baby momma drama."**

Wayne and I exchanged numbers and so did my sister and Tom. We went back to the US. I felt St Lucia calling me or was God speaking to me? Anyway, I met a young lady named Jan and she introduced me to Kevin. He was the founder of a community based organization.

He and his team were doing whatever they could to make a difference on the island. I decided to plant a seed in the ministry. I had bought a trunk full of books with me. They were bibles and books for teens and woman and men. Some Christian inspirational books as well. Kevin also worked for the BBC (Boys Training Center). I decided to visit with Kevin. I met the Director and left some books for the boys. I had planned to do ministry there also.

Keith then introduced me to some of his friends. He also took me to the prison and introduced me to the Warden. I was able to donate recovery bibles and other books to the library. It felt great. It was better than a full time job which I had done for many years. I was making a difference in the lives of others. It is better to give then to receive.

Everyone treated me nicely including his wife, family and friends. Kevin had a brother who was incarcerated he wanted to dedicate his life to people who needed a fresh start. Wayne and I found a chance to connect and he took me around the island. He seemed like a nice young man, cute too.

I guess my ego enjoyed his company. Eventually I invited my sister back with me. Jan took us to a non denominational church. I was introduced to Pastor Dennis his wife and family. They treated us very nice and seem to like that we were Americans. They were just starting out so I felt led to plant another seed to help with the office.

My sister and Tom became good friends. I had always been concerned about his heavy drinking. A few years later he died in a car accident on his way home from celebrating his birthday. He was with a friend, and was a passenger. She was devastated, I was in St Lucia and gave her the news. ***Momma said, never feel sorry for a man he may drink too much and not make it home."***

I went home and went back to my life. Wayne and I spoke on the phone from time to time but never about me relocating to St Lucia. Then the day came, when God reminded me of my plan vs His plan. I did not want to hear His plan. It required taking a major risk. But he presented a opportunity for me to make a difference. Which actually I had asked Him for this opportunity now I was backing out. How could I after being so dedicated to a husband that meant me no good?

I decided to travel back to St Lucia again but this time I met a woman on the plane. I showed her a Poster of Kevin's community program the Kevin had given me. She pointed to a picture of the Warden of the prison and said, "that's my husband." I said what? Once again divine intervention.

I knew it was God, there are no coincidences and God not be in it. She was a very nice lady. Her name was Mary. I got back to the villa and there was Jan waiting for me. She was pregnant and asked me to be the God-mother. I thought that was strange since we had only known each other a few months, but said yes, I knew she wanted me to bring something back for the baby during my travels. I did not mind. Because I knew she needed the help.

Jan began to tell me about her marital problems. Her husband was a police officer. She also had health problems fibroids was surrounding the baby. I did what I could to encourage her including prayer and giving her books. She was always very helpful always making herself available.

Jan and I visited the non-denominational church again. But this time I met a young lady named May. She had been in an abusive relationship and had found the courage to get out. I shared some of my story with her and we became friends.

I met the Pastor and his wife again. He did not seem to like it when he realized I had become friends with May. I watched as he put her business out in front of the whole congregation. He spoke of how he had rescued her from her abusive relationship. He seemed way to preoccupied with her business. She watched in embarrassment as he took all the credit.

She and I would sit and talk at the back of the church after service. He would walk up and stand there with this dead look on his face and would not utter a word. I could clearly see that this man had another side to him. My stomach felt nervous. **Momma said, "never feel sorry for a man he may become obsessed with you.**

I went back home to the US and God kept nudging me to go back to St Lucia and move there. I kept arguing with Him. I meant what I said when I told God that I would go where ever He sent me. I was not thinking of relocating to a third world country. God what are you doing? Florida would have been better. I could have taken all of my children with me there. This had gotten complicated.

I had a desire to teach recovery and encourage others. I believe that God has anointed me to do so. I remembered when I first got into recovery, I told the devil I would tell anyone that would listen. God has a sense of humor, although I am still learning. He could keep me focused on my recovery, if I am helping introduce others to recovery.

I had this thing about losing myself in my relationships. Only God could come up with a better plan for me. Of course He knows me better than I know myself. I finally surrendered when God reminded me of how many, "people I could help in two years?" God was right.

I was started making plans to relocate. I had to break the news to family and friends and my mother. My family thought I had lost it. Even my new friend Wayne was surprised about this plan. I felt hurt because I realized that the people closest to me didn't really know me. I really did love God and was going because He had given me a great opportunity to make a difference. *But in reality people learn more about us as we learn more about ourselves and learn to be transparent.*

I had my issues but run from my beautiful new home and leave my family and friends for a man. There are enough men here in the US. I loved my country. That was not my way of doing things. Besides I did not know Wayne like that. I loved my relatives especially my children. Jesus was the man this time.

It was almost funny, some of my relatives from MD traveled for the going away party. They were coming just to see if I was leaving this beautiful house in Voorhees. It had been only four years. They probably were coming to see if I looked crazy. I felt confident but sad and was worried about what everyone thought. For that reason alone I would not have gone on my own will. *My sister in-law was the only one that seemed to understand and give some words of encouragement. It's not about what other's think, its about what God thinks.* **If God be for me, who can be against me?**

It was hard, I had four children and only one was twenty one. I sold the house, purchased a duplex for the two oldest and took the two youngest with me to St Lucia. The oldest was not home most of the time, especially once she started driving. The middle daughter had started having depression symptoms. Thank God that she had good friends there for her. She also believed in God. God told me that it would not be a easy journey.

I had some good times hanging out at the resorts. Then there were times when I felt discriminated against because I was an American. Americans visited the island, but most did not relocate there I later discovered. I would be out getting something to eat and I would be ignored while the St Lucian servers would wait on the white skinned person first. I would hold them accountable for ignoring me, but not in a nasty way, just direct.

Although it was not easy to leave, God knew I could handle it. He had been preparing me all along. I have learned that our trials and tribulations in life are designed to show us what we are made of. They also help guide us into our destiny although sometimes we get sidetracked. ***But God works all things together for the good for those who love Him.***

The island is beautiful with it's blue Caribbean Sea water on one side and the Atlantic Ocean on the other side. God is amazing when He creates. I also loved the views as I would drive at higher levels and could look down and see the cruise ships, sometimes four of them in the harbor.

Driving was a challenge; I had to drive on the opposite side and make sure I did not slip into a drain or go over a cliff. I was confident that I could do it with God's help. I loved to drive anyway, probably because I did not get my license until after thirty five. I wanted a new car. Getting my license in St. Lucia was easy since I already had one from the US.

I was thankful that we did not have to take the bus. They were little vans and crowded and stinky. They did not drop you off at your home, so you had to walk up a hill or through some bushes. Most Lucians have strong legs, even the elderly women. They are hardworking people. I admire that about them.

St Lucia's view are breathtaking. I call it the island of hidden beauty, because one minute you are looking at something that looks like maybe a poverty area. Then the next minute you make a turn and it takes your breath away. The views of the Pitons are something I had never seen before. Oceans, mountains, beautiful blue clear skies and peace. This particular side of the island was a whole different vibe then on the north side of the island. Every weekend local parties on the block and some of the blocks you don't want to visit.

I was thinking of our visit to Cancun Mexico which was also a beautiful place to visit. Many of the resorts sit on top of small hills. I love the Mediterranean designs. But some of the men in the tourist shopping area seemed to have a lack of respect for the American women. One actually tapped my sister's butt as we were shopping for souvenirs. I was hoping he did not do that to me, cause I would not have taken it lightly. Every since I was a young girl, I never liked the boys in school trying to get a feel. ***Momma said, "never feel sorry for a man, they may stereotype you."***

In December my youngest daughter and my youngest son had relocated to St Lucia with me. At first they saw it as a vacation because we had to stay at the villa for a few months. The elderly couple that I bought my house from was building another house behind mine. They asked if they could stay until their house was finished. I was waiting for my shipment to arrive anyway, so I said yes. Everything has to be shipped by boat that included my furniture etc.

I had introduced my children to my new Lucian friends and associates and of course Wayne. They loved the beauty of the island and my daughter loved seeing the little children in school uniform. Each school has it's own color. I had to put her in middle school and my son went to private school.

Then reality had set in. My youngest daughter was use to sharing a room with my middle daughter and now she was living on the other side of the world in her room alone. She really missed her sisters. She had problems with some of the Lucian girls at school because they were jealous of her. She handled it well because she has a fiery personality, but deep inside she was hurting and would sometimes call her sister and go to her room and cry.

She and my son did not put up a fight at first because they just wanted to be with me. But after a while I felt like I had let them down. I asked God why didn't he wait to call me when they were older? He said, "trust Me". I just told them that God had a plan and would work everything out for all of our good. They were meeting people from all parts of the world. England, Canada, Thailand, Antigua, Barbados as well as my son was learn to speak the Lucian language while making friends.

I trusted God, but there were times when I missed my friends and family. I was use to going to meetings and things were so different now. We were use to the bigger malls, highways and we missed the choices we had for entertainment. I was use to seeing plays at the Merriam Theatre with my mother and sisters. Going to Christian comedy shows were also my favorite. I also missed my church in NJ including the way my Bishop and Asst. Pastor taught the Word of God.

I missed the family gatherings on holidays and so did the children. We always had a good time. In the beginning we went home on Thanksgiving but after a while we were beginning to miss

Thanksgivings so that we could travel home for Christmas.Although we went home a few times a year it got to be expensive. If you are visiting on vacation there is plenty to do. But when you live on the island you can't behave like a tourist 24/7.

I met more people, some I thought would be friends but many were not as genuine as I thought they were. Integrity and good character was not important to them.They usually had motives. Jealousy was a big character defect. So God gave me good discernment with people. Sadly, most had motives. I was lonely for friends to just hang out with although sometimes May and I would go to the resort and have dinner.

I met a young lady named Joanie during my traveling back and forth. She worked for the bank and was a mother of three.We got along very good and most of all she was a Christian. We met at the airport in Antigua. She was waiting for a seat, I had a ticket but some how we ended up sitting next to each other on the plane.

She probably was the only person that had never asked me to bring her something when I traveled back to the US. She was a little envious and wanted me to put her in my bag as she would say, when we traveled home. I did not feel threatened by her. She invited us to her home and we would relax and pray and hang out with the kids. I really admired how she would have bible study with her children who were very young, and those kids could pray.

The Psychologist and Pastor at the non-denominational church wanted to know all about my connections in the US.Why? I guess to benefit himself. He also tried to keep me close by choosing the children's ministry for me to oversee. That would have been a privilege and I was good with children. I had been praying and asking God for wisdom and guidance. I did not feel led to join his church.

He and his wife asked me to be on their radio program. He said I could say whatever I felt God was leading me to say. I was able to write my own recovery lessons and share over the air waves. I was sharing my experience, strength and hope according to the Word of God, with nothing but the anointing and some knowledge and experience I had acquired. I felt honored that God trusted me to do so.

I have always loved radio and commercials/TV. But would have never imagined that I would be doing it. I use to say that if I had my way I would have been an Entertainer/Actress. I also love Motivational Speaking as well. Kevin asked me to co-host his show with another friend of mine named Thelmie.

He had plans to start a television program, more like a talk show. We met at the station a few times and did a few recordings. Once I arrived with the guest Pastor who was not pleased with how disorganized things were. Kevin wanted to control everything but was not good at organizing.

Thelmie and I offered many times to help him but he wanted to do it himself. I felt God was telling me to back out, so I did, although I was looking forward to co-hosting the program.

Less than a year later, I was on the radio. God had given me favor. I had been praying about my relationship with the Pastor. His controlling behavior scared me. One morning I woke up and God gave me a vision of me doing my own radio program. I said, "oh, no what are you getting me into"? What would they think of me?

I faced my fears and did it in love and told them that I felt led by God to have my own radio program. Too my surprise they took it well and seemed to understand. After maybe a year or so he asked his wife to call me. He wanted me to come back and take half of his program time. I declined his offer.

I know it was God because the program was successful, people loved it. I started off on PrayzFM. I prayed every step of the way for guidance, and God would help me as I chose each topic for discussion. The program's name was New Perceptions. I could not believe that God was trusting me to teach Christian recovery. One program had eventually turned into three. "New Awareness" and "Transforming Teens" on two different Christian stations.

I believe what God says and I love truth. It is important to me that as Christians we grow. Stop the lying and cheating and stealing and pray about jealousy and envy, and anything else that we are struggling with. Be honest with God, He knows and sees everything anyway. He knows our personal struggles. He knows us better than we know ourselves. It's not easy to look in the mirror but liberty is very rewarding.

I have fallen short many times, but I know where my strength lies. I thank God for repentance, grace and mercy. Even as a young girl I hated lying. I believe that as Christians we are to be humble about our strengths and weaknesses. When we miss the mark, be humble and repent. Ask God for help. He loves us as His precious children.

I was on PrayzFM until they closed a few years later. Some of the employees including the manager started another station called RizzenFM and asked me to join them. By this time I had joined up with JoyFM another station. I felt it was work for the Lord, although I believe they were competing against each other. I stayed out of that. I felt the Lord's work was more important and of course what God thought.

I spent time with some of the youth in St Lucia. I felt led to do something for the youth and the prophet that visited us had confirmed it. By this time I was asked to teach the Religious

Class at the middle school. It was volunteer but it was a good experience. We talked about the music industry and how the girls can dress with integrity. We talked about what God thinks about the challenges teens face. We talked about righteous behavior based on a scripture I wrote on the board from the bible.

I asked my son to join me on a program called: Transforming Teens. We informed teens of things that were going on. We also researched some of the challenges that teens have and my son and a guest including myself would do the program. Of course for every program there was a call to receive Christ at the end. The programs gave people hope.

It's been over 5 years and a great experience. I was surprised that so many people loved the programs. I was invited to be a guest on another program. There was times when the devil would tell me that I was not helping anyone; then God would have someone in the Supermarket recognize my voice from the radio. I would thank God for confirmation and press on in faith.

I had met some local Christian entertainers in ministry who were members of the church I had joined called Bethel Tabernacle. They chose to do ministry with me at the community center and at the prison. I had previously volunteered at the prison to speak to the women's group, plan workshops and provide supplies. It was a very interesting and rewarding experience.

My heart went out to the women who were from other countries. They were manipulated by some guy they had fallen for and found themselves in prison because they were smuggling drugs for him. When many of them needed the guy's support he was not there for them. ***Momma said" never feel sorry for a man he may manipulate you and then kick you to the curb".***

The radio programs allowed me to be transparent. God used this to give me favor with many people including the inmates that were listeners of the programs.

Mr. Herd the Warden, let us do a concert at the prison for the inmates. It turned out well and another young pastor from another church that I almost joined agreed to give a Word to the inmates as a favor to me. Mr. Herman wanted us to do it yearly but the money was not available. I had been paying out of pocket although I was able to get a few donations from the businesses in town.

One of my sister's in Christ gave my name to a woman who was in charge of a Cruise Ship Ministry. She knew I would assist and I did. Again I got a chance to learn new things about myself and about ministry on another level. This cruise ship would come to the island with items to give away to those in need. It was like a big cookout in town. Food was served and Christian entertainers came to worship and minister. I felt blessed to assist with the Christian artists and those responsible for such a blessed event.

The local artists that were my new associates from church would make themselves available whenever I needed their assistance to do ministry within the community. I loved the fact that they loved the Lord and was serious about serving Him. My Bishop/Pastor in St Lucia had agreed to help as well. For he had heard of the new ministry I started with God's helps called: New Beginnings Transforming Lives.

I had always expressed love to him and his family when ever I saw them outside of the church as well. I liked him, he is a man of integrity and excellent leadership. He is an excellent Pastor as well and his wife an excellent first lady. His daughter is also our new Reverend; we have this love and respect for one another although we have never gone out.

Funny when I was interviewed at the church she did not have many questions, she felt that she already knew me. She was a listener of the radio program, like I said I was transparent. I had formed a relationship with people over the radio, many I will never meet. The programs were also aired in other neighboring islands. You can also listen in other countries online. Rev. Tashia's dad is our Bishop and making a difference all over the island and other islands. I prayed and asked God for a new church home. I believe God told me to go to Bethel after I had visited a few other churches. Bethel is a Pentecostal church on fire for God.

I was use to the Baptist church, but I gave it a chance. I loved the fire and boldness of the Pentecostal Church in St Lucia. I had learned more about taking authority as a Believer. The Baptist church in St Lucia was loving but reminded me to much of my childhood. That was not a bad thing but I needed more because my mind had expanded.

# Chapter 10

## Marriage #2 Still Growing

Now of course, the enemy had to send a distraction. Wayne was my distraction, but also a lesson for me. As we are helping others God still shows us the areas in which we need to grow or heal. Wayne grew up in a little community called Cul De Sac. Most were very poor. He lived with his grandmother. His auntie and a few nieces and cousins lived down the road.

I saw the house that his grandmother was living in and my heart just went out to her. There was no complete roof, kitchen was not finished and they had no bathroom. Here I came from a country where even the poor had a bathroom. My heart just went out to his grandmother.

She and I developed a special bond, although most times we could barely understand what each other was saying. Some times Wayne had to translate for me. She was a strong little lady as far as I could see, although she developed cancer and died a few years ago.

Before she died, I decided to finish the house for her including painting it a beautiful apple green color. Her eyes lit up with so much happiness. I felt blessed to be able to do it. She was the talk of the community, and some neighbors were jealous of her blessing.

I thought people who worked for the resorts were paid very well. Sadly to say some foreigners start businesses in these countries and pay the employees very little money. It appears to be a way of taking advantage of those already less fortunate.

Finally my container arrived and I was able to put my furniture in my new house. It was not as nice as the one I had in NJ, but it was a nice house for the area I was living in. I decided to paint it a beautiful caribbean green. The gate was painted red. My art work looked beautiful in the house. I had no regrets but I did miss my large walk-in closest.

I also decided to get two Rotweiler puppies. We named them Ocean and Sky. They are great dogs and loyal to their owners. They are in the Working Dog Class. I recommend them highly for pets. They are territorial, love their owners and great home protectors. You don't have to train them to be vicious just love them and make sure they respect you.

Wayne asked me to be his girlfriend. Deep inside I knew it wasn't a good idea but I said yes. It was the start of another relationship that would mostly cause me grief. We traveled to Antigua and Barbados. While in Barbados he began to act strange and irritable. He slapped me when I had done nothing to him. I could not understand his change in behavior. He took the rental car and drove off. He was gone for a few hours.

I was feeling confused and angry and hurt. He returned happy as if he did not remember slapping me. He appeared to have been drinking. He was going on and on about a nice couple that he had met. They seemed to have satisfied some type of need.

Why was I even spending time with this man? Of course, he apologized and I forgave but I was not ready to let go of this relationship as of yet. Why?? *"Momma said," never feel sorry for a man, he may abuse you and pretend nothing never happened. You may choose denial over self-love.*

Wayne made himself more available and *I was happy to have someone available for me and the children.* I decided to do something that I said I would not do. I allowed him to move it. Now what was going on with me? I later realized an old issue had resurfaced. Or shall I say I still had some underlined pain to deal with from the first marriage.

My sister and I had vowed that after our first marriage we would never allow a man that was not our husband to move in with us. Things were going well for a while and then here comes baby momma drama. His ex-girlfriend seemed to always be in the picture. She was also co-dependent and would use his son to control him if he allowed her to.

She still had feelings for him although they had broken up some time ago. I would pick up Wayne from work and his disposition had changed. I mean when he left for work he would be calm and happy. He was distant and did not talk about his feelings by the time he got off work.

One night I let him drive home and he was strangely quiet, almost like the calm before the storm. I asked him how work went and what was bothering him? Instead, he stepped on the gas speeding up the hill. I was afraid wondering if he would kill us both. I said, "ok ok" and he stopped. I could not understand the rage.

Apparently, I later found out that he was being teased by co-workers about our relationship, that included our age difference. We both pretended that it did not bother us but in reality it did. We wanted the relationship to work for whatever selfish reasons we both had. *"Momma said" never feel sorry for a man, he may suppress his anger"*.

You know co-dependents push important things under the rug, or suppress it hoping that it goes away. Meaning sometimes not accepting reality and not setting heathy boundaries. *That also includes compromising standards and accepting sex for love.*

Wayne started doing other things such as lying to me and smiling in my face and walking out of the door and coming back late at night. I later found out that he had had an affair with a teenage girl. Sometimes I would walk into the bedroom and he would be on the phone whispering. Of course when I confronted him he would say it was his mother or a relative. I knew he was lying. *"Momma said, "never feel sorry for a man he may disrespect you in your own home."*

I would hold him accountable, but in reality I had committed too much of myself too soon and was afraid to let go. I felt trapped although I had choices, self deception is the worse deception.

In the meantime, my children knew the relationship was in trouble and they began to act out. My daughter was living with us at the time. She saw the rage and it all got to be too much for her as she watched him throw his temper tantrums. I later found it that his behavior took her back to her childhood when I was with her father.

She missed her sisters as well and asked if she could move back to the US and I said yes. She had been there over a year. I later found out that she had gotten pregnant during a recent vacation to the US. She is now the mother of two children. Sadly, I can see Coda issues in all of my children. Actually, I believe these behaviors is why Jesus died on the cross for us. God knew we would all have some kind of personal struggles, whether we label it or not. The list of Coda issues are long and many can identify with some of the characteristics. Although most won't admit it. Many are learned behaviors.

Wayne had tantrums when he felt he could not control. He carried a lot of guilt and condemnation. He also was very wounded from his childhood. He had been abused by his father who was a police officer. He spoke of how his father treated him as if he was stupid even trying to enroll him in a school for retarded children he abused him by beating him and giving favoritism to his younger siblings. This was because he had a very short term relationship with his mother.

He tried to make things right with me by coming clean and getting counseling. He got his Visa and went to the US to a Co-dependency program. It appeared he had gotten some kind of breakthrough. We decided to get married after I gave him a chance to choose between his old life and the life he had with me. Of course he proposed. ***Momma said, "never feel sorry for a man, he may ask you to marry him knowing he is not ready to be a husband".***

I went in town and rented a dress because things were so expensive in St Lucia. My family did not have the money to fly over. I invited most of my friends and associates from St Lucia. My friends from the US could not make it either although I did not tell many of them. Our reception was at Bay Gardens Resort. We got married at our church on the island by our Bishop. We had gone to counseling but did not continue. We had broken all of the rules. ***"Momma said, never feel sorry for a man, he may not want to do marriage counseling."***

In reality I had moved away from my comfort zone in the US and did not want to be alone. I had once again compromised myself and my children were once again involved in my mess. ***Why?***

**Subconsciously, Deep down inside I was afraid. I had trusted God enough to make the move to St Lucia but had not trusted Him to take care of us while we were there. Because of my childhood trauma I have always struggled with fear. Being in a relationship was my security blanket. Momma said, "never feel sorry for a man, you may compromise because you are fearful and don't want to be alone."**

I had a friend named Jerry from my church in St Lucia. He was very young but very wise. He called me mom, but to me he was like a little brother. I loved him and his mom. Before I was foolish enough to marry Wayne, my friend Jerry use to listen to me, watch me cry and then pray with me and encourage me. Sometimes he even spoke to Wayne. Of course, Wayne's pride got in the way. He would only speak or call Jerry when he got desperate, meaning when he thought I was going to put him out.

Five months after Wayne and I got married things got worse. His son came to live with us and was jealous of my son. He began to do vindictive things like slash my son's bike tires. He jumped off of the dresser while my son was watching TV and purposely landed on his knee. Something he had seen another boy do to another kid at school. He sat on the floor one night while my son was sleeping and destroyed his video games one by one. There were several of them, my son would collect them during our travels back and forth to the US.

What a nightmare, things were crazy, my son woke up and wanted to hurt him but chose to go into the bathroom and cry instead. He understood that he was older than my step-son and did not want to hurt him. My step-son was maybe 8 at the time.

Wayne actually accused my son of breaking up his own games. That goes to show how his thinking was. (As a man thinks in his heart so is he). I had made some foolish choices. I knew something had to change. I was so angry with myself that I began to feel as if things were hopeless and then depression reared it's ugly head in my life once again. My son was acting out and so was Wayne. *Momma said, never feel sorry for a man, he may mistreat your children too."*

One day, Wayne was going through some drama with his son's mother. It had been going on for some weeks. I knew it was just a matter of time before he exploded. I tried to talk to him but he kept smiling and holding on to the anger. He did not handle pressure well. He had gotten some help, but did not have a heart change. He deceived himself into believing that he was delivered from his past. *Momma said, "never feel sorry for a man he may tell you that he is already well in his mind."*

I took my son for a day at Windjammer a resort with villas. We were with his friends and their parents. We were having a great time sitting on the beach. They loved my spiritual nature. But they said that they were of a Bahia religion I had never heard of. I believe they worshipped the profits of the bible. She had met a man named Moses and he misled her and her sister into this so called faith. *"Momma said," never feel sorry for a man, you may find yourself worshipping the wrong God".*

I received a call from Wayne, he sounded strange. My stomach had such a nervous feeling in it. He insisted that we come home. I was afraid and waited a while. Then I decided to go home. He came out of the bedroom in a quite rage. He asked for the key to my SUV. I pointed to the table. I told him that I did not understand his behavior. He needed to do whatever he felt he had to do.

I was standing in the kitchen next to the microwave. He looked at me and began to yell. I don't know what he was yelling about. He picked up a insect repellent can and came down hard on my shoulder blade with the sharp end. I felt a burning sensation on the bone of my shoulder blade, my feelings went numb from the shock. That is another coping mechanism from people who have suffered abuse or trauma of any kind.

I told him that he was not going to get away with it. He yelled some more and walked out of the door. I called the boys out of the room.

I grabbed some clothes for the boys. I called the police but they did not take me seriously. The cab showed up first. I dropped my step-son off to his grandmother. I knew Wayne and his mother would be looking for him. I took my son and we checked into a resort hotel. *"Momma said," never feel sorry for a man you many need to take your children and leave your home."*

This was my birthday week, what a present? I wanted him out of the house. Although we were at the resort I did not feel safe. I wanted all of this to be over; I had to clean up this mess. *Momma said, "never feel sorry for a man he may lose control and hurt you or worst even murder you."*

On Monday, I went over to the police station to file for a restraining order. I did not trust the police on the island I had heard horror stories of rape and violence against those they were suppose to be protecting. But I trusted God and went anyway. I told my story to the officer and he gave me the documents to take to the Family Court.

The police arrived at the house to serve Wayne the restraining order. He was always worried about what the neighbors were thinking. Now he had given them something to talk about. The officers did their job, although he knew some of them. They watched as he moved his things out of the house. *"Momma said," never feel sorry for a man you may suffer much embarrassment."*

I had a work house on my farm so he went there. I should have sent him back to his grandmother's. But I knew he would choose to go to the farm first. At the time, I just wanted him out of the house. He was use to the farm because he was use to working the land. We shipped bananas to England every two weeks as another form of income. "*Momma said, never feel sorry for a man, he may have the nerve to stay on your property.*"

This incident had bought back so many memories from my childhood. The feelings of trauma was back. I remember my mother taking us when we were small one night and going to a friends house near by. I remember darkness, flashing lights, fire trucks and sirens. I remember fear; this was after Mr. Kenny had set the house on fire.

I did not want to go back to the house so we stayed at the resort for a few days. I sent for my son's best friend who lived near by to hang out with him. It felt strange felling as if we were sneaking to his home. We had to look out for the dump truck that Wayne drove, hoping he would not pass us on the road. I did not want to see his face.

When we arrived back at the Villa, I sat on the beach thinking about my life my choices my son and of course my crazy marriage.

I did not come back to the house until I knew he was out. It felt strange going back. By now my step-son was with him at the farm. His mother was not happy about the situation. Because she had left him with us while she attended school in the US. My son was with me.

Because of the restraining order we had to go to court. He looked like a fool before the magistrate. He could not deny anything. The judge ordered him to go to a men's anger management group at the Family Court house for some months.

I was so embarrassed, because before all of this happened, I was doing my volunteering as a Missionary and getting to know those who were in charge of the Family Court system. I was suppose to help with the Women's Group. Now I was actually apart of the group. **Momma said, "never feel sorry for a man, you may end up a member of the group that you were suppose to be helping."**

My step-son went to live with his mother in the US. I was so grateful. He and my husband both were difficult to live with. He did not want to share his dad with anyone. He had no compassion that my son's dad had died not that long ago. I was a good step-mother to him, I treated him as if I had given birth to him. My son did the best he could to be a big brother, forgiving over and over again. Funny before all of this my son wanted a little brother after living with three big sisters. I am sure he felt different after all of this.

It was awful feeling like a victim again. All because of fear, loneliness and the fact that I had *chosen to love a man that I felt sorry for.* His childhood and environment had been traumatizing too. He of course did not appreciate all I had done for him and the love I had shown to his family.

He was selfish and arrogant and prideful with a capital P. He lied and cheated and abused me. Was it all his fault? NO. But everyone has to look in their own mirror. God deals with us all individually. **Momma said, 'never feel sorry for a man, he may walk all over you and not appreciate you." We must teach people how to treat us. Don't accept unacceptable behavior from them nor yourself.**

*In reality, I had set myself up by not keeping the standards I had set for myself.* I had allowed fear, insecurity and loneliness to control my life once again. I felt like a victim; I had to get away. I booked a flight and my son and I went to the US for maybe five weeks.

I had a life in St Lucia and commitments so I decided to return. I started going to the Women's Group for abused women at the Family Court. I had to get back on track. I had to find myself again. I had to take responsibility for the choices that I had made. He started going to the Men's Anger Group. The groups met on certain days, so I was able to avoid him. I was beginning my healing process.

The Administrator of the Family Court liked me and knew who I was from the radio program. She allowed me to volunteer and speak to the women's group. Sometime experience is the best teacher. I lead the group as needed for a few months. It was a good experience although during this time I was still having a lot of anxiety. I was giving out but not getting back. I needed to step back and take care of me. *Momma said, "never feel sorry for a man, it may take some time to get rid of the fear."*

I decided to start family counseling with my son. It was difficult because he was angry with me and had lost some respect. The therapist had her own private practice not far from our home. She had attended school in the US and spoke English well. She had grown to like my son and I. We would have been good friends had she not been my therapist, so we had to set boundaries.

She had to keep reminding my son that he had a good mother, but not a perfect mother. I chose to humbled myself and apologized for my bad choices. But I would never apologize about moving to St Lucia. I knew it was a God given opportunity to make a difference. I was doing that. Now my marriage was a different part of my life, like another scene in a play, more like a soap opera.

But of course with him being young he did not understand and could not separate the two. All he knew is that I had taken him away from his home in the US and now look at our circumstances. *Momma said, "never feel sorry for a man it may affect your relationship with your teen/child."*

I had not seen my husband in eight months and he appeared to be doing well at the men's group. For some strange reason I wanted to see if he had changed at all. I would not let him come to the house. We began to meet at the coffee shop. We talked and he seemed to be doing well. He was humble and eventually went back to church. He also started Family Counseling and we did Couples Counseling.

My last husband use to call me the little engine that could. I thought it was a compliment all those years ago. Thank God *the mindset can change*. I had this thing about staying in unhealthy relationships too long. I kept thinking maybe things would get better. Because I had married him I held myself accountable by trying to prove to myself that I had done all I could do.

I still believe that we should do all that we know how to do before letting go because marriage is to be taken seriously. **Momma said, "never feel sorry for a man, you may not let go soon enough". You may even rationalize why you should stay and continue to be used and abused.**

Eventually we had started seeing each other on the weekends. We were also still in Couples Therapy, the sessions got intense at times. She told my husband that he had a good wife with some flaws and that his behavior was triggering my insecurities.

She would find herself getting frustrated with Wayne because of his cheating. During our time apart he had cheated with a seventeen year old girl. Seeing him at all was not a good idea right. My Pastor from the US, later told me on FB that I needed to give my husband time to show me a level of maturity and consistency. That was confirmation from God.

I had asked him the question and he gave me a wise answer. I had been watching his program "On Point". I was so happy that I could see him all the way on the other side of the world. These programs helped me come back to myself. In other words helped me get my thinking back on track. The fearful issues were beginning to fade again. I started seeking healthy support systems while on the island. I also went to church but did not share my personal business with the members. I was still doing the radio programs.

I was able to use some of my experiences on the radio, because I did not want anyone to go through what I had been through. Only God can use you while He is still challenging you to GROW. I felt unworthy at times, but then I remembered that I was only saved by grace and with a willing heart God can do whatever He wanted to do.

My husband and I did the weekend thing for over a year and I found myself getting so frustrated. I was not seeing what my Pastor in the US had told me to look for. I could not understand while one minute we were reading our bibles together on the balcony and the next he was acting as if he had never done it. I held him accountable by saying why the change? He began to argue with me and accuse me of trying to control him. ***Momma said, "never feel sorry for a man he may think accountability is control."***

I did not want to control him, but I did need stability. It took sometime and a lot of frustration. I finally heard the Holy Spirit speaking to me, He told me that my husband had been pretending again. He had not had a heart change. He did what he felt he needed to do to get back into my life.

It was amazing to me because he had joined up with me doing ministry. I was in the community center in the area where he was raised. I was teaching and sharing my experience, strength and hope. He was beginning to slack in that area as well. He had made many promises to support what I was doing and then backed off more and more. ***Momma said, "never feel sorry for a man he may not be a man of his word."***

He was beginning to show up late and some time not at all. He was beginning to make up excuses as to why he could not make it, again the Farm and work came first. A argument we had on a regular basis. One evening he showed up bible and all. I was already at the center. He had prepared a lesson. I spoke first as he patiently stood by the wall waiting for his turn. I could tell something was not right with him. I watched.

I was sitting at the table audience facing me. He sat down with his bible and began to speak. My spirit was uncomfortable. He seemed to be acting in his own strength. I got confirmation in my spirit. I was given a word, "Fake" came up in my spirit. He seemed to be putting on a performance. He was speaking and as he was talking he looked over at me held out his hand as if it was my turn to dance expecting me to finish his word for him.

I could barely look at the faces of the audience. I had also bought my son's friend there for the first time. I was watching as he and my son began to whisper as I watched the people there seeming discontent. I held my head down as if I was reading the bible or what ever he was referring to. I could not wait until he was done. The word "fake" just kept coming up in my spirit. ***Momma said, "never feel sorry for a man he may not be genuine.***

I did not say anything, I began to observe and pray for more revelation. He had went to the Farm. My son and I started talking. He told me that his friend asked him if the guy that was talking was his step-dad. He said, "yes". and he said, "he is a fake. Well I was done. God had confirmed what I heard in my spirit. I told my son about my revelation as well. It was a sad moment. ***"Momma said, never feel sorry for a man, he may be desperate enough to fake it."***

How could I marry someone that was almost opposite of me. Yes, we loved art and beautiful things and some types of music. Yes, we loved some of the same colors. Yes, we were both affectionate. Yes, we loved the ocean and dogs and trucks. Oh, and he cooked and cleaned. I liked that about him. He wasn't bad looking either. He was intellectual and spiritual sometimes. I was at the point where I did not know what was real and what was fake in him anymore. I did not trust him being around . . . *finally.*

**Fact:** *We also both had trauma issues and the character defects that comes with it. THINK.*

But how could I forget about values and Godly character. I hated lying always did and he lied with no conscious. He cheated, and laughed and set me up to think everything was good between us as he planned to take my vehicle and meet other women. I felt it in my gut that something was not right. I just did not understand the smiling face. "**Momma said, "never feel sorry for a man, the things you have in common may not be as important as good character." His smile may not be genuine.**

We were constantly arguing about his selfish ways, and he appeared to be blind by his own pride and selfishness. He wanted and wanted it was all about him. God had also shown me that through the counseling and other help given to him; his heart and mind was made up. He was not going but so far, he was doing just enough to get what he wanted.

I held him accountable by telling him what I knew, and giving him the chance to do what was right. He usually confirmed everything by is prideful attitude. He told on himself after a while. *I got tired of arguing about the same things over and over and over again.* Sound familiar?

I realized I was hitting my head against a brick wall. In the back of his mind, accountability was the same as control. He was not going to let anyone control him, forget all the dvd's we watched on how to have a healthy family and all the other teachings and TBN programs we had watched, his mind was made up. *Momma said, "never feel sorry for a man he will do just enough to get him over."*

What do you do when you have done all you can? Are you thinking of, Donnie's song, "Stand"? Ladies, there are men in the world that are good hearted and there are some that are not healthy enough emotionally, spiritually and mentally to be in a relationship with you especially marriage.

Many see marriage as a trap, some see it as a way to get only their needs met. Some men just don't want to be lonely. *Momma said, "never feel sorry for a man"* he may marry you for Selfish reasons.

Some women marry for selfish reasons as well, as I did. What was my reason? I did not want to be alone in a strange place so far away from home. I had forgotten that I was not alone; God promised to *never* leave me nor forsake me. I had the Creator of the Heaven and Earth with me. He is my Almighty protector. I had my Heavenly Father with me. I had Jesus, my Lord and Savior with my children and I. I have a God with me that sees me as valuable. I am always on His mind. *Amazing how easy that comes to me now.*

God revealed to me that I answered the call when He gave me the opportunity to relocate to St Lucia. But then after all I had gone through to get there, there was still parts of me that needed to die to Self. Fear and insecurity was still deep inside of me. I trusted God to get me there but I did not trust Him to keep me.

I was suppose to lean on Him when I relocated but instead I backed away and once again came up with my own plan. It has been said, that God laughs at our plans. Old Co-dependent behaviors had surfaced once again they had creeped up on me like the snake in the Garden. I too like Eve had begun to reason.

I was not loving myself, although I had loved God enough to go . . . and do His work. I was some day hoping to have a mate that would serve God with me. I did not expect that in St Lucia. But instead I felt alone once again with my children as I always had even in my previous marriage. **Ques: How do you feel like a single mother when you have a husband? Answer: Marry a selfish man.**

My daughter had stayed over a year and then went back to the states. My son was still with me. I did not have all the answers, I just went. I wanted God to lay out the whole plan. If he did I may not have gone, especially if he had told me that I was going to suffer more. Actually, He did remind me that things would not be easy since I was going for Him.

The depression had hit me so hard at one point I thought I would not come out of it. But I knew better than that. God would help me, and I am a fighter. Until this day, I am grateful to God for bringing me out. It felt like the devil and I were at war. He wanted to destroy me, he wanted me to kill myself. I felt as If I would go crazy. I would lay hands on my own head and anoint it with oil. He wanted me to give up.

I was so numb and angry and resentful that I could not shed a tear. I desperately wanted to cry. I even remembered trying to make myself cry. But only the pressure in my chest and the anxiety seemed real. I remember it so well. I refuse to go back to that deep dark hole again. I had prayed and prayed and spoke the Word of God. **Momma said, "never feel sorry for a man you may beat yourself up and think yourself into depression".**

Like TD Jakes said, you gotta use what you got to defeat the enemy. I knew a lot. I knew I had to use my weapons of warfare unless I would surely die. My TV stayed on TBN most of the time. I went to church, I listened to my Pastor in the US and in St Lucia. I watched dvds and listened to cds in the car. I prayed with a friend. But I was not giving up. **Momma said, "never feel sorry for a man, you may have to fight for your lif**e."

I flew to the US and went to a retreat in Chicago. It was a retreat for people who had Codependency Issues. It was a plane ride and also a hour and a half bus trip. I received a lot of love and acceptance. The people there could not believe that I had traveled so far for the retreat because many of them were local. The bus stopped at a hotel and then I had to take a taxi. I was late but some were up after 10pm just socializing and volunteering for late registration.

When I arrived, I met a nice lady who heard I was coming because I had called and told them that I would be late, she put some food in the fridge for me. Then I was shown to my room, it was like staying at a college dorm. But I did not have a roommate. I put my things away, got my food and sat at a table in the kitchen with one of the Chaperones.

We introduced ourselves and talked a while. I hate to eat a lay down, and some of the people at the retreat was taking a walk around the camp grounds. I decided to go. It was dark with many trees. I decided to go back because I was tired. I went to my room, I had my own bathroom I liked that. I read, prayed and spoke to God and trusted that I was safe and went to sleep in this strange place in the suburbs of Chicago.

I got up the next day and showered. Then I received a phone call. It was from Wayne, my husband. I don't remember much of the conversation. But I do remember him trying to push my buttons. He was angry because I had left. Unfortunately, I allowed him to get under my skin. Then began to get angry and emotional. I decided to hang up after feeling the anger rising up in me. I did learn a lesson from that experience.

I learned that once again I had given him power over my mind and emotions. I learned that I had went away to start my healing process and I did not need to speak to him. So during the remainder of the retreat worked my recovery by setting some boundaries. I chose not to speak to him. *I chose to put myself first for a change.* **Momma said, "never feel sorry for a man, he may try to upset you when you need peace more than anything in the world."**

I was feeling anxious but got ready for breakfast and the workshops. I went downstairs. I was on the second floor. I went outside, it was beautiful. There was a small lake and a walking trail and park area with benches. Some people were sitting under the tree reading, some were taking a walk. I love nature. When I was a teenager, we use to live near the park in Philly near the Zoo and I would carry my folding chair to the Park with a book and just sit there for hours.

Some was just socializing by the dining area. I went in to have breakfast it was set up buffet style. There were some Youth attending their own retreat. This place was connected to a church the teens attended. They were just finishing up their meals. Then our group sat at the tables and got to know each other. Most were loving and friendly and smiling and having fun.

The sun came through the window, I felt it's warmth. I felt I was in the right place I felt safe. I was grateful to God for being with me. It was like when I went to Florida, I just knew God was in the midst of my recovery process. He had guided my steps. This worked for me, but I know that as a Christian some of my fellow brothers and sisters in Christ would not understand. My relationship with God is personal and so is His plan for my life. He meets us where we are and gives us what we need. I am grateful to a God who is so loving and understanding.

By the way these retreats are not part of a cult. We tend to criticize and fear what we don't understand. I am blessed to have my church family and my recovery family. Although, I do pray for those who are in recovery who have not yet accepted Jesus as Lord and Savior. I pray for everyone that has not accepted Christ including those who have backslidden.

Many have gotten the revelation that He is the Higher Power in the program. God wants us to get recovery regardless of how it is introduced. We need our minds renewed in many ways and the self-destructive behaviors must change. But lets never forget the Word of God. Most meetings end with the Lord's prayer or the Serenity Prayer.

## Serenity Prayer: *long version*

*God grant me the serenity to accept the things I cannot change, the courage to change the things I can and the wisdom to know the difference. Taking each day one day at a time, living life one moment at a time accepting hardships as a pathway to peace taking this sinful world as it is and not as I would have it, being reasonably happy in this life and forever with you in the next. Amen.*

I was a little skeptical when I finally surrendered to God about writing this book. I have always worried about what other people thought of me. But if this book helps anyone to make better choices and change behaviors or save a life, then it is worth it. *For if God be for me then who can be against me?* I have broken my anonymity, but only for Jesus. As God is helping us we can help others as we grow.

My Pastor reminds us that God wants us to not be self-centered and to pray for others. God already knows what our needs are.

We fasted and prayed for others although I have done so in the past, but I didn't leave myself out. I thought that was great. During those bible study times I could feel God delivering me as I placed the names of people on the alter on Wednesday evenings at Bible Study.

I had been a compulsive eater since my childhood. When did it start? It probably started during the times of abuse that was going on in my home when I was very young. I felt helpless and powerless. I wanted to help my mother so bad I even thought about taking the abuser's life. My father was somewhere drinking and feeling sorry for himself. He was not one of the abusers that was in my mother's life. They came after. ***Momma said, never feel sorry for a man, you may leave the pitiful alcoholic for the sicker abusive alcoholic instead."***

One night after fasting and bible study was over. We stood in a circle around the church and Bishop prayed. I got in my car to go home. I decided to not go out to eat. I had made up my mind that I would have a almond peanut butter and jelly sandwich and go to bed. Usually I would let my mind tell me what to do. But this time was different. I was growing and my mind was changing. God is delivering me. He was waiting on me to surrender my will. He does that you know.

Sometimes I am not patient with my own recovery, but I have chosen to take God's hand of grace and not look back anymore. I can do all things through Christ which strengthens me. He is a very present help in the time of trouble. He is my joy and my salvation whom shall I fear or dread. The joy of the Lord is my strength.

The fellowships I attend is a good place to be to get what I need. There is acceptance and respect among people who are complete strangers. It's important to set healthy boundaries in all types of relationships. Like they say, everyone is not your friend, although you may have some things in common with them. It takes time to really get to know people. But on another note I have also met some life long friends.

The retreat was filled with support group meetings that allowed me to get back in touch with my feelings again. I love how organized it was. There were topics for each need. We had our agenda and just like a convention we chose a topic and headed for our class. My breakthrough did not come overnight but It was a one day at time process. After all it had been some years.

I tell people the Missionary part of my life in St Lucia was great, but the marriage part was a big mistake or major lesson. *Momma said, "never feel sorry for a man you may live with regrets".*

I was given the tools that I needed. Some of the tools were the slogans. So simple and easy to use if I chose to use them. Such as: easy does it, first things first, let go and let God, Think, this too shall pass, one day at a time, and a few others. Focusing on the steps and the principles behind them also helped me to focus. This also included my Bible: there is Power in the Word of God and I quoted those scriptures until I finally got my breakthrough.

For me it all worked together. I was a tough case and God knew it. Actually, I speak to God and quote scriptures daily over my life and the lives of my love-ones and friends. I pray if an ambulance passes me by. I pray for anybody that God lays on my heart, even strangers I see.

That also includes my enemies and those who have disappointed me and hurt me. It's the right thing to do. It's the healthy thing to do. Forgiveness is for my peace of mind too. Can't give that away because of pride.

The retreat was a safe place to share and not be judged for my insanity. Actually, that is something I wish the churches had more of. Unfortunately, there is still too much self-righteousness and judgmental attitudes in the body of Christ. Some people just don't want to admit that they have issues.

We tend to forget that we have more in common than what we care to admit. Recovery is not just for alcoholics and addicts. Although we become addicts to our own stinking thinking. It's what led us to seek a Savior in the first place. What a man thinks in his heart so is he. There is no competition just a loving God's help. His ways are not our ways, His thoughts are not our thoughts.

My favorite part of the retreat was the bonfire. We sat outside after dark, in a circle as the fire blazed to heat us. I believe it was maybe October. Some had blankets and looked so comfortable. Each person raised his or her hand to share their experience, strength and hope and victories. I say that because some people think that self-help groups only talk about the bad stuff. It's exposing the stinking thinking and getting in touch with the feelings.

We also talk about the changes and healthy choices that were made when we could have done just the opposite. We also talk about the solutions and God's goodness. We all learned from each other and the experience was memorable. A time to get away from it all sometime is healthy.

The retreat was very beneficial. It was like pieces of me was slowly finding their way back to me. My feelings were still all over the place and peace was still a stranger but I received bouts of it. I was fighting to take back my power that I had lost in the marriage. **Momma said" never feel sorry for a man you might lose yourself in the relationship."**

*I had gained over twenty pounds since* my relocation to St Lucia after committing myself to this relationship. I had more scars from the physical slaps in the face and being hit on my shoulder blade with a insect repellent can. I had emotional scars from the horrible things he would say to me. It's just by the grace of God that I am writing this book.

I have learned to ask God for strength and He has been faithful. I have learned how to be humble enough to lay my issues on the table before God as he reveals them to me. I am not ashamed to ask God to remove anger, resentment, pride, insecurity, confusion, arrogance or anything that gets in the way of me loving God, myself, or others. I pray for my enemies or people that hurt me. I have learned to forgive, I choose to forgive no matter the circumstances. I just do what God says do.

I was raised by a single mother who did not know how to give up, it paid off in negative ways but also in positive ways. She is strong even today, recently recovering from cancer saying that she refused to believe that she was going to die.

Unfortunately, she is still in pain everyday after being a victim in a transit bus accident in Chester PA a few years ago before she was diagnosed with cancer. I am sure she is walking around numb. Where do you think my shortcomings came from? So much as happened to her.

I could not understand why that part of my life was not over. I loved God and just wanted to get on with my life, but not another dysfunctional marriage! God also revealed to me that I had not healed from the last relationship.
I

In recovery its been said to go on a relationship fast for a year and work on yourself. I guess I was suppose to work on my relationship with God, pray, work on self-acceptance and self-love. I was too emotionally ruled to go along with that plan.

A year? Sex was not the issue just wanted someone to be there that I felt loved me and to protect me. I had a thing for men that would hold my hand. It was a sign of protection for me. I guess that was the little girl in me that was still missing her daddy. I had always wanted my dad who was an alcoholic to come and protect me and rescue me. I had gone through so much trauma. It's been said that many women still want their daddy's love and acceptance and attention. I also wanted my daddy's presence.

I have seen women who felt they needed to perform to get their daddy's love. Some daddy's just did not know how to show love to their girls. So many women still yearn for the love that their fathers still hold onto or maybe took with them when they left. Some will never get it from their biological dads. That's something that many women will have to accept.

My father is gone, when he was alive a part of me was still waiting. When he died in the 80's I had to learn to let go. I now thank God on his birthday for taking care of him. I hope he got right with God before he died. The feelings and most of all the thoughts of abandonment is gone too. I gave it to God some time ago. *Momma said, never feel sorry for a man, you may stay with him because you want your daddy's love."*

I was in and out of relationships during my two years of partying. My ex-husband died in Aug 2003 and I had remarried by 2006. I was use to running and keeping it moving. It was about the pain .... I did not want to feel it. So much had happened between 1986 up until the present. Let's not mention the trauma from my childhood. I am just talking about my adult life.

I got so use to it, meaning stuffing my feelings, and running, I did not know that I was doing it. I guess some denial was there too, because all I knew was I had to take care of my children. I could not trust anyone else to do it better than me. I had to survive for them.

While in St Lucia, I would slow down to take sometime to forget about my problems and go to the Spa to behave like a tourist although I was living on the island. I was enjoying the beautiful sights of the Caribbean. The views from atop of the roads were breathtaking, looking over the Atlantic Ocean.

Sometimes I would book a room at the resort. But it was nice just visiting for the day and going back to our home. My son was always with me with his best friend or friends. It was nice watching them enjoy themselves as I sat by the pool or in the restaurant. This was one of my favorite things to do. **Momma said, "never feel sorry for a man, you may not be able to feel your feelings."**

I needed to feel; I needed to feel the disappointment and accept the anger I had towards myself and those who had hurt me. I needed to do some soul searching and accept myself as being human. I needed to hold myself accountable for my bad choices. Of course I could not blame everyone for my stuff. I had another bad habit and that was beating up on myself, it was self-hatred for not being perfect enough. Perfection, another illusion many of us carry around in our heads.

I hated seeing people bully others in school and even today. I refuse to deal with bullies, but I will set boundaries and pray for them. I do not accept unacceptable behavior from myself nor from others anymore. But I am learning to lighten up on myself. God loves me unconditionally.

God had to work with me and he is still working with me. How could I be so giving and loving and accepting of others, and not like myself? Now that is insanity. I am glad to say that compared to how I was in the 90's I have come a long way. At that time I was blaming and controlling and judgmental, critical and filled with fear and disappointment everyday. I wanted to kill something and it was not me.

**Momma said, 'never feel sorry for a man, because you never want to lose yourself or beat yourself up so bad that you could get lost and not be found.** *But God* can find you because to Him you are worth looking for or shall I say like the lost sheep worth coming to get.

# Chapter 11

## The Lessons

"Never feel sorry for a man". We as women must set standards for ourselves in our relationships and follow through. I had done it and forgot I had standards once fear or some other issue from my past kicked in. Let's not forget we all have issues. I love women who refuse to accept that they have issues but can see the weaknesses of others and then sound as if they are bragging about their perfections. Isn't perfectionism an issue as well?

How many times have I beat myself up because I wanted to be perfect? No one is perfect. For all have sinned and fallen short of the glory of God. Romans 3:23. Make sure your standards are not too high, this will take Godly wisdom and discernment. If they are too high and you don't leave room for another persons' character defects then you can run a good person away from you. Love is patient but not desperate and too needy. I said too needy because we all feel needy sometimes, its apart of being vulnerable to those we love.

If you like myself took some time to get it, meaning you are now over 30, don't give up. Seek first the Kingdom of God and His righteousness and He will give you the desires of your heart. Those who have suffered much sometimes get caught up with the suffering. Pain is inevitable, but suffering is optional. We can learn to make better choices and think better thoughts.

Never feel sorry for a man, we all have a past and many times it is not pretty. We can't change the man; he must see himself as lovable and willing to change. We feel sorry for them when we hear their sad stories. But we must remember that we *didn't cause it and can't cure it.*

Instead it should be a red flag that he might not know how to love you because he did not have the proper up ringing and does not love himself. He may not trust women that could be a major issue as well. Now you have to suffer because of what some other women did to him.

Maybe his mother wasn't there for him and he has abandonment issues. Maybe he feels his mother was a whore and all women are whores to him. Men have low self-esteem too. He needs his own personal relationship with God. Don't forget you do too.

The world's way of doing things do not work and is not permanent. Meaning, dressing seductively to get a man, he will just use you and give you a label. You know men label women right? What category would you like to be in. Forever, freak or friend? Says one of my favorite authors: Michelle McKinney Hammond. How many women say they want to be friends but still give too much too soon?

How many women say wife, but do not behave as wife material. Having sex before marriage, or shacking up together just makes things more complicated. God does not bless the so called union. Then you begin to make him choose to marry you quickly because of guilt or insecurity. This is an insane way to try to fix it. He get's pressured and then both of you end up miserable. Some men are selfish enough to go along with it, or some break your heart and walk away. Some even marry someone else.

We can deceive ourselves into thinking that we have everything under control, when in reality it is just reasoning and our perceptions are not seeing the reality of the circumstances. **Please don't waste time waiting for a man to change.** I have done it and even today I see other women doing it. Sadly to say just because he does not live with you does not mean you are not desperate. You may be compromising instead. How much of you have you given to him? Then there is the man that has been married before and does not tell you that he does not want to get married again. You wait hoping he will change his mind. You deserve better.

Then there is the secretive man, the non transparent man. Have you met his family? I am not talking about a cousin or an aunt. Does he take trips and most times you don't go with him? Does he disappear for some strange period of time and just reappears like Houdini? He tells you that he went to NY or something, like my ex-deceased husband use to do? LOL. I can laugh about it now, but it was not funny at the time. I am sure he had women all over the place and children that I have never met.

There is the woman that has committed herself to the man and some years have gone by and now he won't commit. She has made some changes for him, and he only gives what he wants to give only making promises. Good intentions are just maybes. Some never get a ring and a wedding date and she waits and waits hoping he will come to his senses and sees that she is a good woman. Many men know a good woman but they are set in their ways.

Some get the ring and he keeps postponing the date. He gets irritable when the conversation comes up, or he manipulates by saying he wants to have a big wedding and can't afford it or some other excuse. Or he may accuse the woman of trying to control him. Be realistic with yourself, sometimes we don't want to accept reality. *Be a lover of truth no matter what. Let go and let God. God will work all things together for your good. He loves you more.*

A man that does not want to commit can get use to such an arrangement. He has a key to your place and all the other benefits if you know what I mean. He can come and go as he pleases. You sit there lonely as he secretly does what he wants to do behind your back. He has studied you he knows just how to get you back on his side. He may cook for you or maybe take you on a weekend getaway. He may buy you something to put a smile on your face. The wrong man can manipulate too. So why should he commit? Once again, we women set ourselves up for disappointment and denial is not a river in Egypt.

Then there is the women that trusts no man and is so desperate that she decides she wants anyone's man. Insanity, he will never leave his wife for you and if he does, do you really think you have a winner? Insanity, self-deception is the worst deception. How many women have told themselves, "although he cheated on her he won't do it to me?" She deceives herself into thinking she is the better woman.

Then there is the women that treats the man as if he is a little boy or her son. He complains and acts like a rebellious child. Sometimes she gets tired of being his mommy. But in reality do you want to raise a man? Let his mother do that and God can help him grow up. That is not your job. *Momma said,' never feel sorry for a man, and take on the role of his mother."*

I recently asked someone, this question. Do you think waiting for him to change could be in the way of your destiny? Do you think those bad habits that you don't want to face could be in the way of your destiny? You were born for a specific purpose. If you don't believe it, then that is proof that you need all the help you can get. God said you were and He does not lie.

If you don't believe in yourself then why are you waiting around for someone to change and you need to change as well? He does not treat you right and you don't treat yourself right. Ask yourself does he support your destiny? Don't compromise out of desperation. Ask yourself why do you compromise? Learn to be honest with yourself. Listen to your own internal dialog. When you speak to yourself are you uplifting yourself, or are you secretly putting yourself down, and blocking your own success?

Do you secretly tell yourself that you are stupid, ugly, never going to get a man, will always fail? What are you saying to yourself? Are you your own worst enemy? If so pray and do the work to help your mind get renewed. God is downloading new revelation you must be willing to change. God will give you courage.

Are you the woman that is married to her job? But then pretend you are not lonely or jealous of other women? In reality, you don't trust you have made some promises to yourself that may be stopping you from attracting the right man. Fear may be controlling your life.

We must learn to walk consciously and not as fools. Then we go around and blame EVERYTHING on the man, but ladies we must take personal responsibility for our behavior as well. Do you want to get healthy? We must give God our mind, that takes practice, but we can start by doing what he tells us to do no matter how uncomfortable it is. Cast down those imaginations. We must learn to THINK differently. We must learn to work our way out of the corner we have blocked ourselves in.

The old ways are not working. That includes: manipulating with anger or sex or self-pity. Be honest about any type of unhealthy behavior, if you want to be free. Ask God to help you get out of your own way. Many women are controlling, I heard a woman that I know closely say she is not controlling and she is one of the most controlling women I know. I also realize that she is very insecure about other women. It is very important to get to the root of our dysfunctional behavior. Do you want to run a good man away?

Controlling women are very fearful women, she tries to control everything and everyone around her to make herself feel secure. Then there is the thought of suicide for some women. Maybe she falls in love to quickly out of the fact of being in love with love. You don't want to FALL in love you want to choose to love the right person. It is a choice.

I recently was watching some of the YouTube videos of Phyllis Hyman. What a sad story. I saw a beautiful women who was so insecure about who she was. She was tall and beautiful. But on her interviews she usually spoke of not having a man or she would put herself down on live TV in front of the whole world. That was so amazing to me.

She sang like an angel. She was so talented, but did seem to see enough value in herself. She chose to sing songs that she felt was her real life experiences. In reality she chose to sing songs that kept her seeing herself as a victim of her circumstances and failed relationships. Her mind needed to be renewed. She needed to accept that she was chosen by God with all of that beauty and talent to do His will not her will.

My heart went out to her. If she had learned to **trust** God with her life especially with her relationships things would have been better for her. If she would have taken personal responsibility for learning how to love herself, she would be here today. *Some trust in chariots and some in horses; but I remember the name of the Lord thy God. Ps 20:7*

Someday she would have met the right man. I am sure she probably was running some away because she had such low self esteem. I believe a good man likes a women that is loving and confident. Strong and sees herself as valuable. Although we all have our good days and bad days.

Some women are so comfortable with the soul sick self that they would rather walk around with the low-self esteem. Some would rather wear the mask knowing but not admitting that there is jealousy in their heart and self-hatred. It is self-destruction and needs to be addressed.

Then there are times when we may feel a false sense of superiority and become bullies. The bible reminds us not to think too highly of ourselves as well. We are nothing without God. Everything we are is a blessing from Him to honor is Kingdom.

Never hurt yourself for a man and think you are getting back at him because he hurt you. Once again, self-deception is the worst deception. He will get over you, believe it you will become apart of his past as he learns to go on with his life. ***Momma said, "never feel sorry for a man, you may get caught up in self-pity."***

Ladies, once again, it's time to stand up and take personal responsibility for our stuff. I meet women all the time, and I want to run when I see the jealousy in their eyes. It is sad, because I have so much admiration for them. I respect them and then the envy or jealousy reveals itself, usually in a conversation or some sort of interaction but the green eyed monster shows it's ugly face. I hate jealousy, because it can destroy what could be a good relationship. We must see ourselves as God sees us that is unique individuals, precious and ***one of a kind. Stop comparing . . . stop it!***

A good man hates drama and he can smell a needy insecure non confident woman a mile away. Now there is nothing wrong with wanting a relationship with a good man and wanting to be married. But remember it is very important to guard the heart, because there are men that would love to hook up with you. He may also be willing to take advantage of you.

Ask yourself is he the type of man I want to marry? Does he have good character? Is he a liar and can't handle pressure? Is he jealous and insecure? Is he cheap and selfish? Does he love children? Will he honor you and support your destiny? Does he have anger issues and could be abusive? Is he a dog . . . cheater.

Most and foremost is he a genuine man of God, not just a church goer. Does he know that he was born for a purpose and destiny and seeks God with his whole heart? Is he the right man for you? **Momma said" never feel sorry for a man, he may pretend in order to get what he wants".**

Try praying and asking God to have His way in **all** of your relationships. Sometimes people are not as loving as they pretend to be. God will give you discernment and expose anything that you need to see. Now the key is that you **must be a lover of truth** and want to see it, even if it hurts. The sooner you accept it the less it hurts. I say this because less bonding time can help ease the suffering.

I have learned to do this; it saves a lot of time. God let's me know if I need to adjust the boundaries or accept reality. This person may need to be put in the balcony of your life, or put in the past. This does not mean that you don't love the person, but love yourself more. I usually pray that I not be deceived; I learned that from Joyce Meyer. Nobody has it all together and the enemy is very strategic. **Momma said, "never feel sorry for a man he may be easily deceived and bring you down with him."**

**Try this little exercise:** take out your cell phone, go to your contact list and hit DELETE. It's a great way to save yourself major heartbreak. You have a destiny to fulfill, learn the lesson and move on. If you get lonely, call a girl friend a family member, join a club, ministry. But know your vulnerabilities. Choose wisely the music you listen to, turn off the Phyllis Hyman songs or whatever triggers you. Don't listen to the music from back in the day if emotionally you can't handle it.

Take your time to get to know him, how many woman date a man for two months and thinks that he is the one? Better yet two weeks and is already acting as if she is his girlfriend/wife. This is self-torture. Strong e-motions can get us to move in the wrong direction. You know those e-motions can get us in trouble if we don't question our thinking and accept reality.

We must be mindful of this type of behavior. We must be willing to be honest with ourselves and change the behavior. I remember some years ago during my party days; I would tell my sister if you feel as if you *need* to talk to him as if your flesh is yearning. That is a wakeup call to check yourself because the emotions are out of control.

You know that feeling of waiting by the phone? You just can't wait for him to call you. He hasn't called yet. Now you are feeling insecure rejected and wondering where he is and who is he with? You can't focus. That is so unhealthy and so codependent.

A older male friend of mine told me some years ago, that women see the tell tell signs of a dysfunctional man and still choose to go right under the radar? Why is that? I know it's true, been there and done that.

Could it be that many women want to be loved so badly? Maybe we want someone to make up for the love we did not get from our dysfunctional childhoods. Or maybe we want someone to make up for the love we did not get in the past relationship. For some it's loneliness. Forget it, that is a fantasy. Only God can heal a wounded soul and make you whole.

Just imagine sending off a sweet fragrance, and I am not talking about your perfume. I am talking about a woman that is naturally attractive because she has the love of Jesus in her. She is whole. She loves herself and sees herself as valuable. She knows her worth. We don't have to try so hard, just grow and be ourselves.

We also need to be mindful of how we dress. We don't need to show our breasts. It is so unnecessary. Cover up; it sends off the wrong message while some are trying to keep up with today's styles. There are some women who know exactly what they are doing. Desperation is not attractive.

Women with these issues don't see the value in themselves.

Why do we have such a hard time believing what God says about us? He says that we are fearfully and wonderfully made, created in God's image. Believe it!

So why be jealous of other women? Is it because we think that other women are better than us, look better, smarter? We think that they can steal our man? LOL. A man can't be stolen he is not a thing. He has feelings and can make choices for himself. Live a life of inspiration, don't become a victim of your own circumstances. Don't become a victim of low self-esteem or negative self-talk. **Momma said "never feel sorry for a man because you may see yourself as a victim".**

You are always on God's mind and he has never lied to you. We need to make sure our relationship with God is intimate and excellent and trusting Him with our mind, body, soul, spirit and relationships. He will guide us into all truths. We need to learn how to trust Him in ALL areas of our lives.

I have learned to pray and ask God for discernment and wisdom in ALL my relationships. I ask God to reveal anything that I need to see. I need the Holy Spirit's guidance. To help me guard my heart. In family relationships, male or female, business or social. Sometimes I still get hurt or disappointed in another persons' behavior but I choose to forgive and remain humble. I also pray for a more compassionate heart, because hurting people hurt people.

I ask God to reveal the lessons and may His will be done in all my relationships. This works, because it overrides my irrational thinking and my crazy emotions. I have learned to Stop and Think things through. The crazy emotions eventually submit to the spirit.

Now let's remember when we are not looking then the man will show up. When you stop thinking he could be the one and it has only been a second date then you have more growth in the area of relationships with men. When you stop stressing about your age and you are getting too old and will never find a man, then he will show up. Stop lying to yourself.

Let's focus on the Kingdom of God and pray that God helps us to feel more secure in Him. Oh Peace, Sweet Peace. NO man can give us what God can give us and no one is perfect, so we need God's guidance. Invite Him in all of your relationships. I cannot stress this enough. Remember . . . . pain is inevitable, but suffering is optional.

He knows you better than you know yourself. God loves you with an everlasting love . . . BELIEVE it. He chose you **before** you were in your mother's womb with a special purpose in mind. There is only ONE of you on the face of the earth. *Momma said, 'never feel sorry for a man, you may base how he treats you on how God sees you and then you may see Jesus as just another man."*

# Chapter 12

## *Wisdom, Knowledge and Understanding*

More than once I mentioned a word called "Codependence" and like myself 18 years ago you may have said, what does that mean?

### Patterns and Characteristics of Codependence

These patterns and characteristics are offered as a tool to aid in **self-evaluation.** They may be particularly helpful to newcomers. **Some** of these patterns may or may not apply to you. But you will know which ones you struggle with if you are honest with yourself and ready to change. This takes courage. Be patient with yourself, as you choose to work on changing these behaviors for more healthier ones. **Trust God to reveal and heal.**

### Denial Patterns:

I have difficulty identifying what I am feeling.
I minimize, alter or deny how I truly feel.
I perceive myself as completely unselfish and dedicated to the well being of others.
I lack empathy for the feelings and needs of others.

I label others with my negative traits.

I can take care of myself without any help from others.

I mask my pain in various ways such as anger, humor, or isolation.

I express negativity or aggression in indirect and passive ways.

I do not recognize the unavailability of those people to whom I am attracted.

## Low Self-Esteem Patterns:

I have difficulty making decisions.

I judge everything I think, say or do harshly, as never "good enough".

I am embarrassed to receive recognition and praise or gifts.

I do not ask others to meet my needs or desires.

I value others' approval of my thinking, feelings and behavior over my own.

I do not perceive myself as a lovable or worthwhile person.

I constantly seek recognition that I think I deserve.

I have difficulty getting started, meeting deadlines and completing projects.

I have trouble setting healthy priorities.

## Avoidance Patterns:

I act in ways that invite others to reject, shame, or express anger toward me.

I judge harshly what others think, say, or do.

I avoid emotional, physical, or sexual intimacy as a means of maintaining distance.

I allow my addictions to people, places and things to distract me from achieving intimacy in relationships.

I use indirect and evasive communication to avoid conflict or confrontation.

I diminish my capacity to have healthy relationships by declining to use all the tools of recovery.

I suppress my feelings or needs to avoid feeling vulnerable.

I pull people toward me, but when they get close, I push them way.

I refuse to give up my self-will to avoid surrendering to a power (God) that is greater than myself.

I believe displays of emotion are a sign of weakness.

I withhold expressions of appreciation.

## Compliance Patterns:

I compromise my own values and integrity to avoid rejection or others' anger.

I am very sensitive to how others are feeling and feel the same.

I am extremely loyal, remaining in harmful situations too long.

I value others' opinions and feelings more than my own and am afraid to express differing opinions and feelings of my own.

I put aside my own interests and hobbies in order to do what others want.

I accept or have accepted sex when I wanted love.

## Control Patterns:

I believe most other people are incapable of taking care of themselves.

I attempt to convince others of what they "should think and how they "truly" feel.

I become resentful when others will not let me help them.

I freely offer others advice and directions without being asked.

I lavish gifts and favors on those I care about.

I use or have used sex to gain approval and acceptance.

I have to be "needed" in order to have a relationship with others.

I demand that my needs be met by others.

I use charm and charisma to convince others of my capacity to be caring and compassionate.

I use blame and shame to emotionally exploit others.

I refuse to cooperate, compromise, or negotiate.

I adopt an attitude of indifference, helplessness, authority, or rage to manipulate outcomes.

I use terms of recovery in an attempt to control the behavior of others.

I pretend to agree with others to get what I want.

I am going to add one: Insecurity is a struggle as well as fear, but maybe fear is at the root of many if not ALL of these behavior patterns. God reveals truth. THINK.

Many of these patterns most likely will be connected with your internal dialog or in other words, the conversations you are having with yourself. While you are thinking of others you know or have been in relationship with that may have more than one of these patterns, don't exclude yourself. We attract whats in us or what we enable.

Pray and ask God to help you pay attention more to negative inner voices or negative thinking. Then you can take back your power and speak positive words. I use scriptures to confirm what God says about me.

Affirmations are helpful too. Affirmations affirm who we are. eg. I am God's precious Creation ... chosen before I was in my mother's womb. I am lovable ... I am intelligent; I am not stupid; I am precious; I am caring; I am giving; I am loving. I am forgiving. I am not easily offended. I am capable of accepting and giving love. I am capable of choosing healthy partners. I choose to forgive myself and others. You can always (google)the affirmations that you may need to help you. Keep it simple. But most of all, study what God says about you.

I can't stress enough how important it is to just hold ourselves accountable and **STAND ON THE WORD OF GOD. Yes, it**

**does take all of that! We must open our mouths . . . . and say what God says. We must be willing to do the work of recovery.**

We are to question our thinking? Is it lined up with the Word of God? If my thinking is fear based, then I can choose to use the Word of God to combat it. **The bible says:** God does not give me a spirit of fear but of Power, Love and a Sound Mind. Repeat . . . eventually the mind will agree, and the emotions will calm down. If you are obsessing about someone or some event, admit to God that you are obsessing as God to help. Also, as God to create a you a clean heart and renew a right spirit within you. Stop fighting your feelings, feel them.

**Prayer is also the key:** When my mind is not sound the first thing I do is admit it, and go to my Heavenly Father in prayer. I ask for what I need, and that includes peace, then I thank God for it in advance. I repent when I need to; I forgive when I need to. I ask for guidance and God gives me what I need and sometimes I go to a trusted friend and ask for prayer or sometimes vent. Get it out, learn the lesson and heal.

I keep an open mind because God can use anyone or anything to get His message across to me. God can use someone that appears to be an enemy to bless me and teach me something. Pray that your enemies be blessed and healed and prosper. This has nothing to do with how you feel. Just do what God says, He is watching and many times we are being tested. I have learned to always go to God first. I ask Him to reveal anything to me that may be hard for me to see. **I love truth** although sometimes accepting truth may hurt. You have to learn how to love truth. Then you and I will get the Victory.

Many of these behaviors are dealt with by doing just the opposite of what we would normally do. You know? The learned behavior.

Once we humble ourselves enough to accept which ones are apart of our own dysfunction we can choose to change our behaviors.

God commands that we love Him, and love our neighbor as ourselves. By the way your neighbor is anybody that's not you. In reality, that is the challenge here, learning how to love yourself, God and having healthy (relationships)with others. This has been my experience. In healthy relationships we can be ourselves, and we also learn how to set boundaries and not let others walk all over top of us.

When we learn how to make healthier choices in our relationships we can expect a miraculous change in our lives if we are willing to do the work that it takes to change these behavior patterns. Many people will not fulfill their destinies because they are not teachable. Pride is a terrible thing. The bible says: My people perish for lack of knowledge. My experience says: we perish for lack of refusal to use the knowledge that God has given us.

## Healthy Expectations:

1. I know a new sense of belonging. The feeling of emptiness and loneliness will disappear.

2. I am no longer controlled by my fears. I overcome my fears and act with change, integrity and dignity.

3. I know a new freedom.

4. I release myself from worry, guilt, and regret about my past and present. I am aware enough not to repeat it.

5. I know a new love and acceptance of myself and others. I feel genuinely lovable, loving and loved.

6. I learn to see myself as equal to others. My new and renewed relationships are with equal partners.

7. I am capable of developing and maintaining healthy and loving relationships. The need to control and manipulate others will disappear as I learn to trust those who are trustworthy.

8. I learn that it is possible to mend-to become more loving, intimate and supportive. I have the choice of communicating with my family in a way which is safe for me and respectful of them.

9. I acknowledge that I am a unique and precious creation.

10. I no longer need to rely solely on others to provide my sense of worth.

11. I trust the guidance I receive from God and come to and come to believe in my own capabilities.

12. I gradually experience serenity, strength, and spiritual growth in my daily life.

CoDependents Anonymous, Inc. All rights reserved.

*So ladies, the answer to your man problems and other relationship problems could be linked to Codependency. Are you making good choices? Are you loving yourself? Are you accepting reality? Have you really given your life to Christ? Are you tired of being depressed and feeling powerless? Do you see yourself as valuable? Are you feeling sorry for that man? Are you enabling him, in other words, doing things for him that he should be doing for himself. Are you holding him accountable? Note: this is not controlling him.*

**Question:** *How does one get healthy relationships with oneself and others, if one does not have the desire to change?*

## ACTION

*Step Four-Made a searching and fearless moral inventory of ourselves.*

*Step four offers me a chance to find some balance. It helps me to identify the things I have been telling myself, and to **learn** whether or not those things are true. Today I will take one of my assumptions about myself and hold it up to the light. I may find that it stems from habit rather than reality.*

*"Let me realize . . . that self-doubt and self-hate are defects of character that hinder my growth."*

*The Dilemma of the Alcoholic Marriage*

**In recovery we take what we need and leave the rest.**

**slogans**

**Live and let Live . . . .** *my experience has been to know what is and what is not my business. There are times when we want to mold others into our image. For example: our husbands . . . children, friends our Pastor. We get frustrated when they don't behave the way we want them to or take our advice. We sometimes don't respect another persons' choices and who they are. Live and let live, gives us permission to live and let go of the things we cannot change. Besides, it's more of God's business.*

**Let Go and Let God**. *my experience: there are problems in our lives that sometimes we just worry about. There are people that we worry about, but when we stop trying to fix it, and let go and let God, then we will see better results. Place those we love in the hands of God . . . .*

and trust them into His care. Besides He is the one that created them. Surrender-Pray.

**Think** . . . We are to stop and **think** about what we want and need to do, if anything at all. We may just need to pray about it. We need to **think** about how to respond to a certain situation instead of reacting which can cause embarrassment or something worse. We need to **think** about things before we do it and question our thinking. Is it an emotional choice or wise one?

**This too shall pass** . . . my experience: no problem is in the center of our lives forever yet we act as if it is. There are also times in our lives when we need to stop and smell the roses enjoy life. We also need to lighten up on ourselves, stop it with the guilt, shame and condemnation. We go from season to season in our lives, we need to appreciate the people in our lives as well. Pray about everything. Cast your cares on Him for He cares for you. Trust Him with all of your heart and lean not unto your own understanding. Prov.3

**Keep it simple** . . . there are times when we overwhelm ourselves with too much to do. We can only do one task at a time. We spend to much instead of counting the cost. It's best to accept the reality of the circumstances. There are times when we say too much instead of using wisdom to defuse the situation. Choose your battles. Work smart. Instead of giving our loved ones speeches, let's try being more direct, and focusing on the bottom line.

**Easy does it:** I have learned that there are times when I need to relax and take a closer look at the situation. Maybe I need to take it one step at a time trusting God along the way. This also helps me to keep the focus on making sure I am taking care of myself and respecting others. Maybe I need to set a boundary and just say no. Maybe I need to rest.

**Let it begin with me:** my experience is: God wants us to learn how to judge ourselves. That is not the same as condemning. We tend to blame,

blame, but it is also best to take a good look at our own behaviors to see if there needs to be any changes. I may need to just ask myself if I am being overly sensitive, or offensive. Am I taking my frustrations out on others? I may need to pray for a person who may be hurting and may have not meant to offend me. It's not all about me. Hurting people hurt people. I may need to set some boundaries with someone who may not be safe. Do not control others. Everyone has a free will.

**First things first:** another one of my favorites, this helps me to prioritize and make sure I am doing what I am suppose to be doing. It is important that I don't allow my e-motions to lead me out of the will of God. Be patient.

**One day at a time . . . .** my experience is that although our thoughts tend to leap into the future during the wrong times, we only have this moment. All problems and situations are not resolved in a day. There are things that we must deal with that sometimes hurt like grief. But if we take life one day at a time and focus on this moment then life is more manageable. Think on things that are good and pure and perfect and lovely. Casting down those imaginations that cause us to fear. Praise God throughout the day in all things.

**These are only some of the slogans. They are tools to help throughout the day. Also the bible tells us to renew the mind and cast down those imaginations that are not healthy for us. Our minds are under attack daily. Sometimes it's just negative learned behaviors. I use scripture, prayer, slogans and of course humility to get me through each day. It works if you are willing to do the work . . . . it's recovery.**

**References:** The Bible, Codependent No More by Melody Beatte. Courage to Change(Al-anon Family Groups) Michelle McKinney Hammond's books are all great. My Pastor: Bishop David G Evans has some excellent teachings that helps build up the spirit and renew the mind. When the Show . . . "Tough Love" starts it's new

Season on VH1 you may want to check it out. I believe it's a great tool as well of learning about Coda issues.

Joyce Meyer did a teaching on Codependency some years ago. It may still still be available on cd. One reason why her ministry is so successful is because she has admitted to the world that she had a lot of problems in her personality that were affecting her relationships. God led her to study the subject.

She humbled herself and chose to go to God with her pain and confusion. He then gave her guidance; she worked her recovery (although she has never been in a 12 step program) with the wisdom and knowledge that God gave her. She was **teachable and transparent.** She was **obedient** and He delivered her. Then he blessed her and her family with one of the most prosperous ministries in the World. She is a women who is fulfilling her destiny. One I admire. One of my teachers.

She admits that some behaviors she still has to practice. I can relate to that. My revelation has been when I am in a crisis, or coming out of one. Some of the behaviors that I have struggled with sneak up on me just like the serpent creeped up on Eve in the garden. The bible reminds us to stay watchful. I have also learned to do Spiritual Warfare if need be.

But thank God for His grace and mercy everyday. He is always available to help us no matter how deep in a pit we allow ourselves to fall into. No matter how bad we feel about ourselves or our circumstances, God is with us. Although we will not be perfected until Jesus comes we still have choices. Even Adam and Eve had a choice.

**God loves us with an everlasting love; He has drawn us with unfailing kindness. Jeremiah 31:3**

Most of our emotional problems and negative thinking problems would go away if only we can get a GREATER REVELATION OF HOW MUCH GOD LOVES US. We can choose to take those thoughts captive. We would have a lot more peace in other words. Imagine being his babies and He is just looking at us with so much love in His heart. When we mess up He is there to pick us up and help us. He is compassionate. Slow to anger with plenty of mercy. We get our hands spanked sometimes because He does not want us to touch what could hurt us. His love for us is perfect. There is NO other love like the Love Of God.

Begin to look for God showing you His love everyday even in the little things. Thank Him every time you see favor, wake up in the morning and arrive home safe. You are safe in His arms. Your family is safe in His arms. Remember God also loves those we love too . . . even more because He created them.

**That is one of my greatest desires without any doubt accept God's perfect love. Let's strive for it . . . . that is the gift of recovery.**

*I once saw my Pastor tell the church to stand up and shout "Recovery"! I thought that was awesome. I know that God came to the earth to help us recover from sin. It is about recovery. No more denial about self.*

**If we make an effort to master these scriptures most of our recovery would be taken care of. Of course there are day to day challenges. But we do have the tools . . . all we need to do is USE them.**

1. *Trust God, Conqueror the negative mindsets, knowing who we are in Christ and accepting it. No Doubt! Facing our fears and taking authority over the enemy even if that enemy is me. Facing the self and holding ourselves accountable. Being confident and humble and let's not forget prayer, praise and worship.*

*Practicing the new behaviors . . . . practice . . . . practice . . . . practice . . . . master.*

QUOTE BY RAMONA: **The Holy Spirit is the coach of my spirit and my spirit is the coach of my mind, will and emotions; together Spirit to spirit we win.**

*Quote by T.D. Jakes: Lord, help me with me.*

**Scripture references:**

**Romans 14:19** *Let us therefore follow after the things which make for peace, and things wherewith one may edify another.*

**Prov. 4:23** Guard your heart with all diligence; for out of it flow the issues of life.

**2 Corinthians 10:5** Casting down imaginations, and every high thing that exalts itself against the knowledge of God, and bringing into captivity every thought to the obedience of Christ.

**Phil. 4:13 I can do all things through Christ which strengthens me.** I am ready for anything and equal to anything through Him who infuses inner strength into me, I am self sufficient in Christ's sufficiency. (amp bible)

**2 Timothy: 1:7** God has not given me a spirit of fear, and timidity, but of power, love and self-discipline. (amp bible)

**I John 4: 18** There is no fear in love, (dread does not exist),but full-grown(complete, perfect) love turns fear out of doors and expels every trace of terror.

**Romans 8:37** I am more than a conqueror through Christ who loves me.

**Hebrews. 10:35** So do not throw away your confidence it will be richly rewarded.

You must see yourself as valuable and willing to make the necessary changes to become the successful person/Christian that God created you to be. We are living in the days where God is sorting out those who are serious and those who are not serious about their lives as a Christian. We can't fool Him, and we can't expect the rewards and all the victories without first committing ourselves as a living sacrifice holy and acceptable unto Him. We must love honesty, honor and dedication just as our Heavenly Father.

**Walk Humbly.**

If you have read this book and have a desire to change but have not accepted Jesus Christ as your Lord and Savior I invite you to do it now.

Repeat: **Lord I believe that you sent your Son Jesus to die on the Christ in my place. I accept Jesus Christ as my Lord and Savior and I give you my life. Lord change my heart, save my soul, heal my mind and help me grow and step into my destiny. In Jesus' Name amen.**